THE
Beginner's
GUIDE TO
Faith

ADRIAN S. JACKSON

A wholly owned subsidary of TBN

The Beginner's Guide to Faith

Trilogy Christian Publishers A Wholly Owned Subsidiary of Trinity Broadcasting Network

2442 Michelle Drive Tustin, CA 92780

Manufactured in the United States of America

10 9 8 7 6 5 4 3 2 1

Library of Congress Cataloging-in-Publication Data is available.

ISBN: 978-1-63769-506-7

E-ISBN: 978-1-63769-507-4

DEDICATION

I dedicate this book to our heavenly Father, our Lord and Savior Jesus Christ, and to those who are seeking ways to help them live by faith and to those who are looking for ways on how to strengthen their faith. I also would like to dedicate this book to my lovely wife, Chanda, and all our kids because they are truly a blessing from God to me. Also, I want to dedicate this book to the brothers who stayed faithful to our prison Bible study and all the guys that came who were in transit to hear the Word of God. Lastly, I want to dedicate this book to all the volunteers that came to preach and teach the Word of God. There are a lot of men and women that came, but Mark and the ministry that he and his wife do to help get working girls off the street is major to me. Also, John Davis from Freedom Way Church helped me to see and understand who I was in Jesus. I would like to say a special thanks to Hershell Fuller and Mr. Chambers for the work they do as well.

If you are reading this book, then that could only mean one thing, and that is God has led you to read this book, so this book is for you. I want you to go ahead and sign here, then show your friends that this book, which is filled with the Word of God, belongs to you.

TABLE OF CONTENTS

INTRODUCTION

Introduction

Why a book on faith, you may ask? Well, I will be happy to tell you. It all started on May 4, 2016, when I was indicted and arrested by the Federal Government. I did not get a bond, and I was forced to sit in a detention facility until the matter was resolved. I came across many books for me to read at this time because we had a library that was full of books. At the time, I was really into detective-type novels, and I had read two or three, but it seemed as if I was losing interest in them. Then one day, I was in the library, and I came across a Christian book. The first book that I came across was a book on faith, and it was written by Kenneth Hagin. I took the book back to my room, and I began to read it. The next time I went to the library, I found a magazine by Kenneth Copeland called *The Believer's Voice of Victory* (BVOV). I remember thinking, *Are they the same person?* How is it that I was looking for spiritual guidance, and the first two things I found were from two different people who both had the same first name? Then it hit me. Kenneth Hagin's entire book was about faith, and the article that Kenneth Copeland talked about was on faith, and I did not have any idea beforehand what faith was. I had never even heard of faith when it comes to a biblical sense. So here I was asking myself what faith is, where it is in the Bible, and if it is in there, then why I had never heard about it. Then I began to wonder if it is something that I can use or might need one day in the future. Today I know what faith is, why it is needed, and how we need to use it all day, every single day.

The Reason for This Book

This is the reason for this book. There could be others out there like I was, stuck in a trap of the enemy with no means of getting out, but this was all a lie from the enemy. The great part about it was that my heavenly Father had already put things into motion for me. After I read the book and the magazine, I was introduced to Trinity Broadcast Network (TBN) and the Hill Song Channel. There I saw Joel Osteen, Joseph Prince, T. D. Jakes, Ron Carpenter, Joyce Meyer, John Gray, Creflo Dollar, Steven Furtick, Jesse Duplantis, Charles Stanley, and a list of others who were talking about things that were related to faith, and I was blown away. I thank God for what He was doing in my life because it has changed my life tremendously as well as those around me, and now, we all live by faith, for Romans 1:17 says, "For in it the righteousness of God is revealed from faith to faith; as it is written, 'The just shall live by faith.'"

According to what type of Bible you have, it tells us that the just or the righteous shall live by faith. It is repeated in other places such as Habakkuk 2:4 and Hebrews 10:38.

INTRODUCTION

"Behold the proud, His soul is not upright in him;
But the just shall live by his faith" (Habakkuk 2:4).

"Now the just shall live by faith; But if *anyone*
draws back, My soul has no pleasure in him" (Hebrews 10:38).

Now here is the funny part. I knew everything there was
to know about the church. I knew almost all the songs we
would sing; I knew how to bless the offering; I knew how
to usher, and then it hit me. I knew everything there was to
know about church and church services, but I did not know
the Bible or the most important thing; I did not know the
author of the Bible. The Holy Spirit spoke to me and said,
"First, you must know him who wrote the book." I quickly
learned three important things. First, faith is all about believing and trusting in someone, and it would be hard to trust
someone who you do not know, so I had to seek out to know
him. Secondly, He, my heavenly Father, was the only one
that could help me, and that it was impossible to please Him
or receive anything that He has freely given to me without
faith. And lastly, that there was only one way to the Father,
and that was through our Lord and Savior Jesus Christ. So
with Him is where I must start. I quickly learned that in order
to live, you must have faith.

"For in it the righteousness of God is revealed
from faith to faith; as it is written, 'The just shall
live by faith'" (Romans 1:17).

That in order to be saved, you must have faith.

"For by grace you have been saved through faith, and that not of yourselves; *it is* the gift of God" (Ephesians 2:8).

To please Him, you must have faith.

"But without faith *it is* impossible to please *Him*, for he who comes to God must believe that He is, and *that* He is a rewarder of those who diligently seek Him" (Hebrews 11:6).

To walk, which means to live, here on earth, you must have faith.

"For we walk by faith, not by sight" (2 Corinthians 5:7).

So if you would ask the question, "Why a book on faith?" I would tell you if you want to live and please God, then this is the book for you.

Chapter 1

WHAT IS FAITH?

What Is Faith?

What is faith? To make it as simple as I know how, so faith is just trusting and believing in someone or something. We use a form of faith every day without even realizing it. Someone made this chair that I am sitting in as I am writing this book. I did not check to see if the chair could support all 269 lbs of me; no, I trusted that the chair was stable and that it could support me, and it would not fall. The chair is only doing what it was made to do, and that is to support me while I am sitting in it. So in biblical terms, faith is trusting and believing in God. Unlike the chair, God is alive, He can speak, and He wants us to trust Him like we trust that chair. We do not even second guess the chair. So why are we second-guessing God, who created the man, who created the chair? We cannot for a second, ever second guess God. Our example to follow in the Bible should start with the "father of faith" himself, Abraham. Romans 4:19-22 states,

> And not being weak in faith, he did not consider
> his own body, already dead (since he was about
> a hundred years old) and the deadness of Sarah's
> womb. He did not waver at the promise of God

through unbelief, but was strengthened in faith, giving glory to God and being fully convinced that what He had promised He was also able to perform. And therefore "it was accounted to him for righteousness."

Romans 4:19-22

Here we see that God's Word was more real to Abraham than his own body, more real than his wife's body, and more real than how old both of them were. He was convinced in the promise of God, and we, too, must be fully convinced. In order to be convinced, you must first know.

Knowing

Faith starts with knowing. You know what a chair is, you know how a chair functions, and you know when a chair is broken or is about to break. This knowing will dictate how you respond or react to the chair. Well, when you begin to know God, you will know that He cannot lie.

"In hope of eternal life which God, who cannot lie, promised before time began" (Titus 1:2).

You must also know that it is impossible for Him to lie.

"That by two immutable things, in which it *is* impossible for God to lie, we might have strong consolation, who have fled for refuge to lay hold of the hope set before *us*" (Hebrews 6:18).

You will learn how he operates as you spend more time getting to know him.

As it is written, "I have made you a father of many nations" in the presence of Him whom he believed—God, who gives life to the dead and calls those things which do not exist as though they did.

Romans 4:17

You will also find out what He takes pleasure in and what He delights in doing here, on the earth.

"Let them shout for joy and be glad, Who favor my righteous cause; And let them say continually, 'Let the LORD be magnified, Who has pleasure in the prosperity of His servant'" (Psalm 35:27).

"Do not fear, little flock, for it is your Father's good pleasure to give you the kingdom" (Luke 12:32).

Thus says the LORD: "Let not the wise *man* glory in his wisdom. Let not the mighty *man* glory in his might, Nor let the rich *man* glory in his riches; But let him who glories glory in this, That he understands and knows Me, That I *am* the LORD, exercising lovingkindness, judgement, and righteousness in the earth. For in these I delight," says the LORD.

Jeremiah 9:23-24

You will know and understand how much He loves you and me.

"For God so loved the world that He gave His only begotten Son, that whoever believes in Him should not perish but have everlasting life" (John 3:16).

Another thing you will find out is that since He cannot lie, what He says never fails.

"For My thoughts are not your thoughts, Nor are your ways, My ways" says the LORD. "For as the heavens are higher than the earth, So are My ways higher than your ways, And My thoughts than your thoughts. "For as the rain comes down, and the snow from heaven, And do not return there, But water the earth, And make it bring forth and bud, That it may give seed to the sower And bread to the eater, So shall My word be that goes forth from My mouth; It shall not return to Me void, But it shall accomplish what I please, And it shall prosper in the thing for which I sent it.

Isaiah 55:8-11

You will come to know that, unlike the chair, He will never break, and He cannot be broken, for He is all-powerful. The Bible tells us that you can be as sure of God as you are sure of the sun rising in the morning.

> "Let us acknowledge the LORD; As surely as the sun rises, he will appear; he will come to us like the winter rains, like the spring rains that water the earth" (Hosea 6:3, NIV).

Now ask yourself this question: do you ever worry about whether or not the sun will rise in the morning? Have you questioned whether your chair was going to hold you when you flopped down onto it? I don't think you have. Well, why would you second guess what God has said? We must be the same way with God. Your faith in God is something you should never question, and when you can get to that point, then you will truly know what faith is all about. Faith is simply trusting and believing in Him and His Word. We must believe Him and His Word over all of the circumstances, over all of the storms that we face and go through and not even give what He has said; he will do a second thought. We must become so sure of God like you are sure that the sun will rise in the morning. That is how Abraham lived, and this is how we must live. I well explain knowing God more in-depth in chapter 3.

Faith the Substance of Hope

In order to truly live by faith, we have to know what the Bible says faith is. We find a great definition of what faith is in the book of Hebrews.

"Now faith is the substance of things hoped for, the evidence of things not seen" (Hebrews 11:1).

Faith is the substance of things hoped for. Let's stop here for a minute and ask ourselves: well, what are we hoping for? Next, we must ask ourselves: what is our hope dependent upon? The Bible has a hope for the spiritual-minded, and the world has a hope for those who are still carnally minded.

"For to be carnally minded *is* death, but to be spiritually minded *is* life and peace" (Romans 8:6).

"Carnally" means earthly or flesh-minded. This means we are ruled and dominated by our five physical senses, which are touching, seeing, smelling, hearing, and tasting. If something does not fit into one of those five, then we cannot believe that my friend is the way of the world. The spiritual mind is to be led by the spirit of God, which is within you, and to believe God's Word over everything that your five physical senses are telling you. Second Corinthians 5:7 spells it out for us,

WHAT IS FAITH?

"For we walk by faith, not by sight" (2 Corinthians 5:7).

We walk by faith and not by what we see. I will explain this, too, later, but let's get back to what we are hoping for. In the world, I can hope for good success, hope I pass my final exam, hope I run into some good luck, and I can hope that the doctor will give me some good news when I go see him. This hope has no foundation; it has nothing to support what I am hoping for. My hope is not dependent on anything but wishful thinking. In the Bible, the hope that this verse is talking about is the hope that is given to us through the promises of God, and His promises can be found throughout the Bible. Before I go any further, I feel that I must explain the difference between faith and hope.

Faith Versus Hope

Faith and hope work together, but they are also different from one another, as the Bible tells us in 1 Corinthians 13:13.

"And now abide faith, hope, love, these three; but the greatest of these *is* love" (1 Corinthians 13:13).

Remember what Hebrews 11:1 told us about faith.

"Now faith is the substance of things hoped for, the evidence of things not seen" (Hebrews 11:1).

Faith is the substance of things hoped for. Kenneth Copeland put it this way. Hope is the plan that faith carries out. Hope is the blueprint. Hope must be present first in order for faith to produce the outcome. He also states that while hope is the blueprint, faith is the material needed to make the blueprint a reality. You see, hope has something to hold on to, that you can think about, that you can picture when the real thing is not present yet, keyword yet. We hope on the promises of God. His promises are what we hold on to, they are what we think about, and they produce a picture of the outcome based on His promises like a blueprint. Now faith is the works; faith is what puts everything together. Faith is saying I have it now; it is mine because God cannot lie.

Faith believes you have it now and acting as if you have it now. An example would be your job. Your contract is like the promise of God. If it says you will get paid on the first and the fifteenth, then you can hope that because I go to work every day, I will get paid because of the type of contract I have. Well, they may pay you with direct deposit, and you may not even receive a check stub. You know that your money drops at 9:00 p.m. the night before, and you can almost calculate how much should be in your checking or savings account without even checking to see first. Well, faith is saying I have my money now, so at 7:30 p.m. I am in the store shopping because I know without even second-guessing that my money will be in the bank at exactly 9:00 p.m. You don't wait until you see it in your bank account; you act as if you already have it, and we must do the same thing with God's Word. Once you find the promise, act on it, move on it, and talk as if you already have it, then you will become the second part of this verse. You will become the evidence of the promise that could not be seen at the beginning of your trial. You will not be disappointed or ashamed because God's Word tells us we will not be and that my friend is our money in the bank. Romans 5:5 states, "Now hope does not disappoint, because the love of God has been poured out in our hearts by the Holy Spirit who was given to us" (Romans 5:5).

So if I could put it in my own words, I would say hope is our contract with God, which comes from our covenant with Him, and faith is our money that is given based on our contract. I am not saying we must work to get things from God because that is of the law, but we are under grace, which means He has given us everything freely because of what our Lord and Savior Jesus Christ has done and because He loves us that much. I just used hope and faith as an example, compared to working on a job in the natural world to help you as a reader to better understand.

Faith, Based on Promises

Some may ask the question, "His promises about what?" His promises about how you will come out of the problems that you are having. For instance, the doctor may tell you that you are sick, but 1 Peter 2:24, along with Isiah 53:5, tells us that God promised that by Jesus stripes we have and are already healed.

> "Who Himself bore our sins in His own body on the tree, that we, having died to sins, might live for righteousness—by whose stripes you were healed" (1 Peter 2:24).

> "But He was wounded for our transgressions, He was bruised for our iniquities; The chastisement for our peace was upon Him, And by His stripes we are healed" (Isaiah 53:5).

You may say, "Well, I don't understand how this works." Look at it like this. John 10:10 states that enemy comes to steal, kill, and destroy.

> "The thief dos not come except to steal, and to kill, and to destroy. I have come that they may have life, and that they may have *it* more abundantly" (John10:10).

This is what the devil does: he tries to steal, kill, and destroy. In order to do that, he has to get you to believe that your sickness that you currently have is meant for you and that you must accept it. I am here to tell you that it is a lie and that God's Words are true because He cannot lie. Remember Titus 1:2, "In hope of eternal life which God, who cannot lie, promised before time began" (Titus 1:2).

The best example I can give is that people can say bad things about you that are not true, but if you believe they are, you will start living like they are true. Then you will be living a lie instead of living the truth. You are not what that person says about you. In order for that person's words to have any effect on you, you must first believe that they are true. The keyword here is you must believe. This is the only way their words can have any power over you, and this is how the devil operates. He shows you the sickness on your body; you heard what the doctor's report was because he knows (the enemy) that if it falls into our five senses, we will believe it. Here is where faith comes in and says, "Okay, I see what is going on here." It is all a lie, and I will not accept this because God says I am healed, and I believe His Words over what I see and feel. I have to be like Abraham and be fully convinced because God cannot lie. Regardless of what the doctor says, regardless of what the medical report shows, and regardless of what my body says, I know what God said, and therefore, I am hoping for God's promise to become my own. Now, when I pray and make God's promise my own, believing that it is for me, I put myself in a position to receive. I have the promise now, regardless if things have changed or not, and now I have turned what I hoped for into faith.

Final Thought

The promises of God are just like they were when the children of Israel were brought up out of Egypt, but now they are better for us because the Bible tells us that we have a new and better covenant. We, too, have been brought up out of bondage. We were bound by sin, but God has delivered us from the power of sin and gave us eternal life; He has given us His righteousness and all spiritual blessings in the heavenly places through Christ Jesus. What God is also saying is that you must get to know Him; you must imitate His Son and renew your mind with His Words so that you can be able to enjoy all of His blessings. God laid it all out for the children of Israel, and they enjoyed the blessings of the Father until they started doing their own thing forgetting about God and wanting to live like they saw the world living. The same thing holds true for us. Many of us, even though we have been saved and have seen the miracles of God like the children of Israel, still will not believe and trust God, and the only answer that I have for this is two things. Either we really don't know God because we are going by what someone else tells us about Him like the children of Israel did with Moses. Moses knew God, and because he got to know God, he wanted to be obedient, he wanted to honor God, and he wanted to become as close to God as he could because of how God made him feel in his presence. We would be like Moses as well if we would spend more time with God ourselves and experience the feeling of being in His presence.

Most of us have just relied on the preacher or someone else to let us know who God is. So the passion for getting to know Him is very weak because we have not experienced it for ourselves. The next reason is the same as the children of Israel. We want to do our own thing, or the cares of the world are so more important to us than God that we are tricked into believing that when I fix all of my problems, when I get myself together, when all of my bills are caught up, then I will make time for God. Well, I am here to tell you the world will never let that happened. The enemy knows that if he lets this happen, it will be over for him, and that is why he keeps us busy with the things of the world. He keeps us trapped under the things we desire and work so hard to get on our own. Now is the time to find out your promises of God. They are all for you. It is time to let God do the things for us that He says He desires to do. He wrote them down in the Bible just to ensure us that these are the things that He wants to do. In His Word, it is God talking to you. Take God at His Word by believing what He says (this means having faith) and being obedient to His Word, and you will notice a change in your life: your attitude, how you feel, and you will notice that you are living from a place of victory and not one of defeat.

Chapter 2

WHERE DOES FAITH COME FROM AND HOW DO WE GET IT?

Where Does Faith Come from?

Our faith is given to us freely as a gift from God. When you accepted Jesus as your Lord and Savior, you became a new creation.

> "Therefore, if anyone *is* in Christ, *he is* a new creation; old things have passed away; behold, all things have become new" (2 Corinthians 5:17).

The Holy Spirit came to live inside of you, and when He came, He brought you the free gift of faith. God has given us all the same measure of faith.

> For I say, through the grace given to me, to everyone who is among you, not think of himself more highly than he ought to think, but to think soberly, as God has dealt to each one a measure of faith.
>
> **Romans 12:3**

To better explain this, think about your body for a moment. We were born with the same amount of muscles and the same amount of bones. You can't grow more muscles, nor can you grow more bones. The same is with faith. You can't grow more faith, but you can do things to strengthen your faith the same way you can do things to strengthen your muscles and your bones. For our bones, we are told to drink milk. For our muscles, we are told to work out, lift weights, and exercise. Well, when it comes to faith, the Bible tells us how to strengthen our faith. Romans10:17 puts it this way, "So then faith *comes* by hearing, and hearing by the Word of God" (Romans 10:17).

Notice, it says "hearing," meaning more than once. In order to develop big muscles, you can't go to the gym to work out one time and be big like Ronnie Coleman. You must continue to work out, and as you do, your muscles will grow. The more you do—the bigger they grow. Well, we must do the same thing to strengthen our faith. We must continue to hear the Word of God over and over and over so that our faith becomes developed like the muscles of Ronnie Coleman. Like our muscles, if we don't develop our faith, it will become weak. When we develop our muscles, it produces strength to endure things to get things done in our lives, and faith is the same way. It produces the strength for us to believe in God's promises in the best of situations and in the worst of situations. If you don't work out on the bench press with 405 lbs, you can't expect to walk in the gym one day and say, "Put 405 lbs on there; I can do it." You will not do this because you know you don't have the strength to. So if you don't work to keep your faith developed, then when hard times come, do you think you will have what it takes to hang in there long enough until what you are trusting and believing God for manifest in your life? God has done His part; He has given you the faith you need. Now, it is up to you to strengthen your faith.

Hard for Me to Believe

Some people say, "Well, I don't know if I can do that; it is hard for me to believe what I can't see, touch, hear, feel, or taste." Let me tell you that if God has told you to do something, you can do it. Remember, He cannot lie, so He would not tell you to do something you can't do. So like faith, which He gave to you, He has given you the ability to do what the Bible tells you to do.

"And God *is* able to make all grace abound toward you, that you, always having all sufficiency in all *things*, may have an abundance for every good work" (2 Corinthians 9:8).

"I can do all things through Christ who strengthens me" (Philippians 4:13).

These two verses tell us that we have everything we

need to do all of the things God has commanded us to do. Faith is built up when you continue to hear the promises of God in your situation. Well, some of you may say, "I don't know how I can do that, we only have church once a week, and the preacher may not cover my situation." That's fine because the Bible did not say who had to speak it; you just need to hear it.

> My son, give attention to my words; Incline your ear to my sayings. Do not let them depart from your eyes; Keep them in the midst of your heart; For they *are* life to those who find them, And health to all their flesh.

Proverbs 4:20-22

As you read it, say it out loud so that you can hear it. YouTube is full of videos on your situation. Search and just listen when you are at home in the shower, driving to work, or while you are working in the office. Buy a CD or download a sermon that really speaks to you and listen to it over and over and over. Some of you still may say, "I still don't think this will help me to believe." God says it will work; therefore, it will work. Think about this for a moment. You either have done it yourself, or you know someone who has told the same lie for so long that they believe it now. It has become so real to them that sometimes they have to remind themselves this is not true. Well, the Word of God will work the same way. You just keep speaking it and hearing it, and you will begin to believe, and that is when God can move in your life. Faith is giving God something to work with, and we will get more into this later in this book. So, start developing your faith because you will not be able to live without it.

Final Thought

God has made His Word available to us. With technology, we have all kinds of access to His Word. I mean, you can be in Georgia and hear your favorite preacher in California. So, there is no real reason why we are not hearing God's Word. Notice, I said real reason. The devil will produce all types of reasons, but there is no real reason why especially if you want to be successful in your life and if you want to live a life that is pleasing to God. Now that we understand what faith is, where it comes from, and how we get it, we now must begin to start living a life of faith. It is different when we don't know something, but we know God is holding us responsible for knowing, so now that we know, let's put what we know into action. Remember, God said if we do what He says and we are obedient, then He will be everything for us that we need. So, my word for you is the same thing that I have to tell myself sometimes, and that is to get out of God's way. If God needed my help, He would have asked me. I must realize that I am the one that needs His help and that He can only help me if I get out of the way, and I do that by being obedient to what He has said and that I believe that what He says is true.

Chapter 3
THE NECESSITY OF FAITH

Is Faith Really Necessary?

We know that we have to live by faith, "For in it the righteousness of God is revealed from faith to faith; as it is written, 'The just shall live by faith'" (Romans 1:17).

We also know that we must walk by faith, "For we walk by faith, not by sight" (2 Corinthians 5:7).

We cannot be saved without faith, "For by grace you have been saved through faith, and that not of yourselves; it is the gift of God" (Ephesians 2:8).

And we know that it is impossible to please God without faith, "But without faith *it is* impossible to please *Him*, for he who comes to God must believe *that* He is, and that He is a rewarder of those who diligently seek Him" (Hebrews 11:6).

Here are four key examples that show a big necessity when it comes to faith. As I said earlier, faith is based on your ability to trust in someone. That someone is God. If you know a person, then you will be able to trust them because you know their characteristics and their capabilities. If you trust and know a person, then you will be able to believe them when they tell you what they will do. So before we get all the way into the necessity of faith, we have to deal with knowing God on a deeper level first in order to build up our trust in Him, in order to believe in Him and in His Word.

Who Is God

Hosea 4:6 tells us that people are destroyed, and they perish because of a lack of knowledge of who He is.

My people are destroyed for lack of knowledge. Because you have rejected knowledge, I also will reject you from being priest for Me; Because you have forgotten the law of your God, I also will forget your children.

Hosea 4:6

Also, Hosea reminds and encourages the people to get to know God and for people to make it their business to pursue the knowledge of who He is. "Let us know, Let us pursue the knowledge of the LORD, His going forth is established as the morning; He will come to us like the rain, Like the latter and former rain to the earth" (Hosea 6:3).

Now, how do you get to know Him, or how do you get

to know anyone? You get to know someone through spending time with them. We must spend time in God's Word because He tells us who He is in what He speaks. Also, we get to know a person through communication. When we pray, we begin to communicate with God. What we fail to realize is that after we have spoken to God in prayer, we must sit quietly and wait for His response. This is where we miss out on what God has to say because we get up and leave before He even begins to talk back with us. I will only touch on knowing God because this is a lifelong process. Knowing Him and who He is will be the backbone of your faith. It will strengthen your faith when you really know who He is, and you will come to know that even when we are not faithful, He is always faithful because that is who He is. Just talking about getting to know who God is would be an entire book by itself; therefore, I will only touch on the subject to help you develop your faith.

A Relationship with Your Father

First, we must know that He wants a relationship with us. That is what you and I were created for. John 15:16 says that we did not choose Him but that He chose us.

"You did not choose Me, but I chose you and appointed you that you should go and bear fruit, and that your fruit should remain, that whatever you ask the Father in My name He may give you" (John 15:16).

We were chosen to be God's children and to be joint-heirs with Christ. John 1:12 says if we receive Jesus by faith, we have the right to be a child of God.

"But as many as received Him, to them He gave the right to become children of God, to those who believe in His name" (John 1:12).

"And if children, then heirs—heirs of God and joint heirs with Christ, if indeed we suffer with *Him*, that we may also be glorified together" (Romans 8:17).

Here are a couple of verses that tell us that we are the children of God, and we cry out to Him as "Abba Father."

For as many as are led by the Spirit of God, these are sons of God. For you did not receive the spirit of bondage again to fear, but you received the Spirit of adoption by whom we cry out, "Abba, Father."

Romans 8:14-15

But when the fullness of the time had come, God sent forth His Son, born of a woman, born under the law, to redeem those who were under the law, that we might receive the adoption as sons. And because you are sons, God has sent forth the Spirit of His Son into your hearts, crying out, "Abba, Father!" Therefore you are no longer a slave but a son, and if a son, then an heir of God through Christ.

Galatians 4:4-7

Behold what manner of love the Father has bestowed on us, that we should be called children of God! Therefore the world does not know us, because it did not know Him. Beloved, now we are children of God: and it has not yet been revealed what we shall be, but we know that when He is revealed, we shall be like him, for we shall see Him as He is.

1 John 3:1-2

So not only do we have to get to know Him as God, we have to also get to know Him as our heavenly Father. Don't it make you feel good that you now know that God, Himself, chose you to be His son or his daughter! For the most part, we have never known that in His eyes, we are His children, so we have not sought out to have that father-son or father-daughter relationship. Jeremiah 9:24 tells us that those who know Him will know that He delights in exercising His loving kindness, judgment, and His righteousness.

But let him who glories glory in this, That he understands and knows Me, That I am the LORD, exercising lovingkindness, judgment, and righteousness in the earth, For in these I delight, "says the LORD.

Jeremiah 9:24

James 4:8 tells us that when we draw near to know Him, He will draw near to us to make Himself known. He is waiting to build that relationship, but He will not force it on us.

"Draw near to God and He will draw near to *you*; cleanse your hands, *you* sinners; and purify *your* hearts, *you* double-minded" (James 4:8).

Colossians 1:15 tells us that Jesus is the image of the invisible God.

"He is the image of the invisible God, the firstborn over all creation" (Colossians 1:15).

The He that they are talking about in this verse is Jesus, so when we look at Jesus, we will be looking at our heavenly Father. Let's take a look at Matthew 11:28.

"Come to Me, all *you* who labor and are heavy laden, and I will give you rest" (Matthew 11:28).

Here we see Jesus telling us to come and follow Him for

us to come and look at His life and to come and understand who He is because when we know Him, we will know our heavenly Father. He also tells us to come to Him to rest. In Hebrews 4:11, it tells us to labor to enter into His rest, and Hebrews 4:3 tells us that those who entered in did so by simply believing, and we, too, must simply believe.

> "Let us therefore be diligent to enter that rest, lest anyone fall according to the same example of disobedience" (Hebrews 4:11).

> "For we who have believed do enter that rest, as He has said, 'So I swore in My wrath, They shall not enter My rest,' although the works were finished from the foundation of the world" (Hebrews 4:3).

That is what faith is all about. When we labor, meaning work, to get His Word in our heart to believe, we will be able to rest because we trust Him to do the work for us, and we don't have to go out and do anything because we don't have the power to; because if we did, we would have already gone out and done it. We must come to Jesus because when we come to Jesus, who is the living word of God, we will see how God wants to treat us by how Jesus treated us when He walked on earth. The promises of God are His Words, and Jesus made His Words come to life so that we may have faith in the written word of God. We must believe. If we don't believe, we will never enter into His rest.

"So we see that they could not enter in because of unbelief" (Hebrews 3:19).

God wants us to enter into His rest, He wants us to have the best, and that best is His kingdom, and it is His good pleasure to give us the kingdom. Remember Luke 12:32.

"Do not fear, little flock, for it is your Father's good pleasure to give you the kingdom" (Luke 12:32).

We must know that it is our heavenly Father's good pleasure to give you and me the kingdom. In Exodus 15:26, God tells us He is the God who heals, not the one who makes us sick.

and said, "If you diligently heed the voice of the LORD your God and do what is right in His sight, give ear to His commandments, and keep all His statutes, I will put none of the diseases on you which I have brought on the Egyptians, For I *am* the LORD who heals you."

Exodus 15:26

Deuteronomy 8:18 shows us that God said He is the one, no one else but Him, who gives us the ability to produce wealth. He is not here to cause us to be poor.

"And you shall remember the LORD your God, for it is

He who gives you power to get wealth, that He may establish His covenant which He swore to your fathers, as it is this day" (Deuteronomy 8:18).

When we look at Leviticus 26:6, we will see that God said He would grant us peace, and in Leviticus 26:9, He said He would look on us with favor. That means He is a God who wants to bless you, heal you, prosper you, love on you, and build a relationship with you. I don't know about you, but that is the God I want to know and love because He first loved me.

> "I will give peace in the land, and you shall lie down, and none will make you afraid; I will rid the land of evil beasts, and the sword will not go through your land" (Leviticus 26:6).

> "For I will look on you favorably and make you fruitful multiply you and confirm My covenant with you" (Leviticus 26:9).

God Is Our Friend, Not Our Enemy

Remember John 10:10, where it tells us that the thief, the devil who is your real enemy, only comes to steal, kill, and destroy. Now, look at the second part of this verse where Jesus said He has come that we may have life and have it more abundantly.

"The thief dos not come except to steal, and to kill, and to destroy. I have come that they may have life, and that they may have it more abundantly" (John10:10).

James 2:23 tells us that Abraham, who was a servant of God, was also a friend of God.

"And the Scripture was fulfilled which says, 'Abraham believed God, and it was accounted to him for righteousness.' And he was called the friend of God" (James 2:23).

Can you believe that God wants to be your friend? Think about that for a moment. Our heavenly Father, the Most High God, who is the most powerful being in all existence, wants to be your friend and not your enemy. Praise the Lord, for He is good, and His mercy lasts forever! For the lucky ones who do have a true friend or two, you know that you can talk to them about everything, and you know that they will just about do anything for you. Notice, I said just about anything. How many of them would die for you? The reason I asked that question is that Jesus did, and He is our best friend. In John 15:13-16, it tells us He laid down His life for you and me, His friends. Wow! Jesus said that we are His friends. Jesus says He will tell us everything that His Father, who is our heavenly Father, has told Him.

Greater love has no one than this, than to lay down

one's life for his friends. You are My friends if you do whatever I command you. No longer do I call you servants, for a servant does not know what his master is doing; but I have called you friends, for all things that I heard from My Father I have made known to you. You did not choose Me, But I chose you and appointed you that you should go and bear fruit, and that your fruit should remain, that whatever you ask the Father in My name He may give you.

John 15:13-16

We must get to know Him so we can be His friend so that He can share the things He plans on doing in the world with us. In Genesis 18:1-3, it shows us that God came to visit His friend Abraham.

Then the LORD appeared to him by the terebinth trees of Mamre, as he was sitting in the tent door in the heat of the day. So he lifted his eyes and looked, and behold, three men were standing by him; and when he saw them, he ran from the tent door to meet them, and bowed himself to the ground, and said, "My Lord, if I have now found favor in Your sight, do not pass on by Your servant."

Genesis 18:1-3

Then we see in Genesis 18:17 that God thought about

41

what He was going to do, and then God said Abraham is His friend, so why should He hide from him what He is about to do on the earth?

> "And the LORD said, 'Shall I hide from Abraham what I am doing'" (Genesis 18:17).

Think about the apostle John and how he was able to write the revelations of Jesus Christ. John was worshipping on the Lord's Day when he was given a vision of the end times. God showed him all these things to come, so this is another example of when we are close to God, He will show us the things that He will do on the earth.

> I was in the Spirit on the Lord's Day, and I heard behind me a loud voice, as a trumpet, saying, "I am the Alpha and the Omega, the First and the Last," and, "What you see, write in a book and send it to the seven churches which are in Asia: to Ephesus, to Smyrna, to Pergamos, to Thyatira, to Sardis, to Philadelphia, and to Laodicea."

> **Revelation 1:10-11**

Now in 1 Samuel 3:19, it tells us that God was with Samuel and let none of His Words fall to the ground.

> "So Samuel grew, and the LORD was with him and let none of His Words fall to the ground" (1 Samuel 3:19).

Now that is a true friend. God is there to back up what we say. God is our heavenly Father and our friend, and He does not want to see us fail, sick, broken, or in poverty. He wants us to succeed, to be healed and healthy, made whole, and He wants to prosper us. It is easy to trust a person when you know what their motives are and the reason behind them. His—are simple; He loves us that much. Now, this is important because when you are going through something you may be going through right now, and this is why you are reading this book, just know if it is something that is different than what your heavenly Father does, then it is not from Him. So run to Him because He promises to get you out of that situation because you are not only His friend, but you are His child.

People in the Bible with a Necessity for Faith

Now, let's look at some people that if they did not use faith, they would not have received the promise, and mankind could have been extinct. Without faith, we would not be heirs with Jesus, and we cannot please God.

"By faith Enoch was taken away so that he did not see death, "and was not found because God had taken him," for before he was taken he had this testimony, that he pleased God" (Hebrews 11:5).

"But without faith it is impossible to please Him, for he

who comes to God must believe that He is, and that He is a rewarder of those who diligently seek Him" (Hebrews 11:6).

In verse five, it tells us that Enoch pleased God, and in verse 6, we find out that without faith, it is impossible to please God. So we know that Enoch had to have faith. When we go back to Genesis 5:24, we can find out more about Enoch. It tells us that Enoch walked with God.

"And Enoch walked with God; and he *was* not, for God took him" (Genesis 5:24).

This means that Enoch sought out to know God and because he sought out God, he was rewarded. God took him, and he never knew death. Now in Hebrews 11:7, it tells us that Noah was warned, meaning God told him what was about to happen on the earth, which tells us that Noah must have been a friend of God or that he was very close to God also.

By faith Noah, being divinely warned of things not yet seen, moved with godly fear, prepared an ark for the saving of his household, by which he condemned the world and became heir of the righteousness which is according to faith.

Hebrews 11:7

Even with Noah, we can go back to Genesis to find out about Noah and God. Genesis 6:8-9 tells us that Noah found grace in the eyes of the Lord. Why? Because he walked with God.

"But Noah found grace in the eyes of the LORD"
(Genesis 6:8).

"This is the genealogy of Noah. Noah was a just
man, perfect in his generations. Noah walked with
God" (Genesis 6:9).

Noah built an ark. Ask yourself this question: where
would Noah get an idea to build an ark? God told him about
the flood. Noah could have said, "Look at where we are,
here in the desert, it has never rained; matter of fact, what is
rain?" Noah did not lean on his own understanding; he just
believed God and walked by faith and not by sight. I am glad
he did because if he did not, you and I would not be here
now, and that is what I call a necessity for faith. Hebrews
11:8 shows us a good example of walking by faith and not
by sight. Abraham did not know where he was going, but he
packed up his family and obeyed God.

"By faith Abraham obeyed when he was called to
go out to the place which he would receive as an
inheritance. And he went out, not knowing where
he was going" (Hebrews 11:8).

In Hebrews 11:22, God is so faithful to His Word that
our words will not fall even after Joseph was dead; the words
that he spoke still came to pass even after he had been dead
for over four hundred plus years.

"By faith Joseph, when he was dying, made mention of the departure of the children of Israel, and gave instructions concerning his bones" (Hebrews 11:22).

What he said about his bones, God made it happen.

"Then Joseph took an oath from the children of Israel, saying, 'God will surely visit you, and you shall carry up my bones from here'" (Genesis 50:25).

And Moses took the bones of Joseph with him, for he had placed the children of Israel under solemn oath, saying, "God will surely visit you and you shall carry up my bones from here with you."

Exodus 13:19

Hebrews 11:23 shows us that Moses' parents knew those baby boys were supposed to be killed, but they had faith; they believed that God would work things out for them and their baby.

"By faith Moses, when he was born, was hidden three months by his parents, because they saw he was a beautiful child; and they were not afraid of the king's command" (Hebrews 11:23).

His parents hide him for three months, then put him in the river, and he was found by the daughter of Pharaoh, the same Pharaoh who had charged the people to kill all males born of the Hebrews. But a wonderful thing happened. The daughter had compassion for baby Moses. God is good, but the story does not stop there. We see in Exodus 2:7-9, not only was Moses' life sparred by an act of faith by his parents but his mother was called to take care of her own son and was paid for doing it. This is what God will do when we walk by faith.

> "Then his sister said to Pharaoh's daughter, 'Shall I go and call a nurse for you from the Hebrew women that she may nurse the child for you?'" (Exodus 2:7)

> "And Pharaoh's daughter said to her, 'Go.' So the maiden went and called the child's mother" (Exodus 2:8).

> "Then Pharaoh's daughter said to her, 'Take this child away and nurse him for me, and I will give you your wages'" (Exodus 2:9).

Lastly, Hebrews 11:33-35 tells us that through faith, they subdued kingdoms, worked righteousness, obtained promises, stopped the mouth of lions, and the dead raised back to life again. So I would say that faith is very necessary if you want to live.

> "Who through faith subdued kingdoms, worked righteousness, obtained promises, stopped the

mouths of lions" (Hebrews 11:33).

"Quenched the violence of fire, escaped the edge of the sword, out of weakness were made strong, became valiant in battle, turned to flight the armies of the aliens" (Hebrews 11:34).

"Women received their dead raised to life again. Others were tortured, not accepting deliverance, that they might obtain a better resurrection" (Hebrews 11:35).

Final Thought

Let's start living a blessed life because we see the necessity of faith. We know the necessity of water, but we don't always drink water like we are supposed to. We will wait until we are dehydrated and about to pass out; then, we start to drown ourselves with water. Having faith in God's Word is the same way. We know we need to believe in Him, to constantly eat and drink His Word, but we wait until we are defeated and almost dead before we cry out to Him and believe in Him to help us. Just like drinking enough water daily will allow us to function better all day in the same way, the Word of God will work when we eat and drink of it all day. So get your daily dose of the Word and continue to have faith in what God says before you are defeated, and all you can do is cry out. It is amazing that the way we live. We want things right now, but we will wait till the last minute to reach out to God to cry out to Him after we have tried everything that we know how to do, and we know that when we do this, we end up getting what we need. So why not go to God first instead of making Him the last resort?

It is time for us to open our eyes and see the trends. We get ourselves into things by doing what we want to do or the way that seems right, but it always ends in the same results. We are still stuck, or we have fallen deeper than what we were in the beginning, and now we have no other choice but to cry out to God, and when we do this is when we are saved, we are set free, and we can see the light again. But then we make the same mistake we always make; after He has freed us, we think we got it this time, and we really don't, and we end up in the same situation again. Maybe not the exact same situation, but it is a situation where we have gotten ourselves stuck, and we need Him to get us out. It is time to start trusting Him with everything and to let Him have the wheel. We must let God drive, and we do that by living by faith, trusting that He will not lead us into that deep hole that we always lead ourselves into. Sometimes, it is the work of the enemy, but the majority of the time, it is our own doing, and it is never the doing of our heavenly Father. Think about that before you go on to the next chapter. Are you ready to let Him drive?

Chapter 4

A STEADFAST AND ESTABLISHED HEART

Faith in Your Faith

Mark 11:23 is a must-have verse when it comes to faith.

For assuredly, I say to you, whoever says to this mountain, "Be removed and be cast into the sea," and does not doubt in his heart, but believes that those things he says will be done, he will have whatever he says.

Mark 11:23 5

This is one of what I call the "Mother of Faith" verses. This is the same verse that Kenneth Hagin stood on for God to be able to bring him off of his death bed as a young teen. He did not know much about the Word at that time, but he was given the revelation of this verse, and it changed his life, and it has changed the lives of so many people. It changed the life of Terrence, a good brother that attended Bible study and will always be remembered for his saying, "The doors to the church are open." His testimony about how he stood on this verse saved his daughter's life, and you will read about it later on in this book. Mark 11:23 tells us that faith will work for whosoever. Meaning it is your faith if you use it, so do as Kenneth Copeland says and have faith in your faith. This means to have faith in Jesus, for He is your faith.

> "Looking unto Jesus, the author and finisher of *our* faith, who for the joy that was set before Him endured the cross, despising the shame, and has sat down at the right hand of the throne of God" (Hebrews 12:2).

We must look to Jesus and believe in what Jesus has done, for He is the author or beginning of our faith and the finisher of our faith. What does this mean, you may be thinking? In order to be saved, you had to believe and trust that Jesus (who is your faith, where our Bible faith first started) died, was buried, and was raised on the third day from the dead. So we must believe in Jesus. We must believe what He has done for us and receive it. Kenneth Copeland puts it this way. Jesus is our substitute. He died to give us life; He was made sin to make us righteous. He became weak to make us strong. He suffered shame to give us glory. He went to hell to give us glory. He went to hell to give us heaven. He was condemned to set us free. He was made sick to give us divine health. He was cast out of God's presence to make us welcomed there. All of this is known as the great exchange. So, we must believe that Jesus did all of these things in order for us to have the promises of God. So, our faith will work when we use it because we believe what Jesus did; He did it all for us. Remember, there is no greater love than for a man to lay down his life for his friends. So have faith in your faith.

Establish Your Heart

Mark 11:23 tells us that we must not doubt in our hearts. That means God will establish us through His Word when His Word is established in our hearts. This is our job. We must first establish His Word in our hearts. How do we do this, you may ask? Well, Romans 10:17 tells us that faith cometh by hearing, hearing the Word of God.

"So then faith *comes* by hearing, and hearing by the Word of God" (Romans 10:17).

Let's look at Psalm 112:6-8.

Surely he will never be shaken; The righteous will be in everlasting remembrance. He will not be afraid of evil tidings; His heart is steadfast, trusting in the LORD. His heart is established; He will not be afraid, Until he sees *his desire* upon his enemies.

Psalm 112:6-8

The He that they are talking about in these verses is you and I. We will never be shaken; we will not be afraid of evil because our hearts are steadfast because we trust in the Lord.

Our hearts are established. When our hearts are established, no matter what happens around us, we must stand in and on the Word of God. When you trust God, you will know that since God is for me, no one can successfully be my enemy. When God's Word is established in your heart, God will come and establish you.

> "What then shall we say to these things? If God *is* for us, who *can be* against us?" (Romans 8:31)

> "But may the God of all grace, who called us to His eternal glory by Christ Jesus, after you have suffered a while, perfect, establish, strengthen, and settle *you*" (1 Peter 5:10).

> "For the eyes of the LORD run to and fro throughout the whole earth, to show Himself strong on behalf of *those* whose heart *is* loyal to Him" (2 Chronicles 16:9).

> We must get the Word established in our hearts.

> "Then the LORD said to me, 'You have seen well, for I am ready to perform My word'" (Jeremiah 1:12).

This means that God is looking for His Word to be established in your heart so he can perform His Word.

Establish Your Heart, Renew Your Mind

When you establish the Word in your heart, you will be renewing your mind as well. They work hand in hand. You must first establish the Word in your heart, and then your mind can be renewed; it must be in that order. It is hard to establish the Word in your mind when our mind is subject to change every couple of minutes without having it in your heart, your spirit, your inner you first. See, a lot of people make the mistake of being established in their minds. See, our mind is our thoughts, will, and emotions. This is where the devil attacks us because he knows the mind is what we operate out of. This is why God tells us to renew our minds. See, if the enemy can get you to fear, accept being sick, accept poverty, have disbelief, and doubt God's Word, then we have become defeated. When we are established in our minds and not our hearts, we have no foundation, our mind can change at the drop of a dime, and we will lose every time we come up against any trial. That is why we are to be established in our hearts with the Word of God, which is Jesus. He is a proven solid foundation that we can build ourselves upon brick by brick, word by word when it is in our hearts. The devil knows this and does all he can to prevent us from establishing the Word in our hearts.

The sower sows the word. And these are the ones by the wayside where the Word is sown. When they hear, Satan comes immediately and takes away the Word that was sown in their hearts. These likewise are the ones sown on stony ground who, when they hear the word, immediately receive it with gladness; and they have no root in themselves, and so endure only for a time. Afterward, when tribulation or persecution arises for the word's sake, immediately they stumble. Now these are the ones sown among thorns; they are the ones who hear the word, and the cares of this world, the deceitfulness of riches, and the desires for other things entering in choke the word, and it becomes unfruitful. But these are the ones sown on good ground, those who hear the word, accept it, and bear fruit; some thirtyfold, some sixty, and some a hundred.

Mark 4:14-20

We see that the Word of God is a seed. So every time we hear the Word of God, it is like planting a seed in the ground. Well, our ground is our hearts, and the enemy is trying to come and steal the seed before it can grow roots. Think about this. It is a lot easier to pull up a plant that has no roots, or its roots don't run deep, but when a plant is rooted deeply in the ground, you can pull all you want. We have to be rooted in Him, meaning Jesus Christ, the Word of God.

"Rooted and built up in Him and established in the faith, as you have been taught, abounding in it with thanksgiving" (Colossians 2:7).

"That Christ may dwell in your hearts through faith; that you, being rooted and grounded in love" (Ephesians 3:17).

Notice that besides being rooted in Him, what other word in these two verses is the Word "faith." So in order for our faith to work, we must be rooted in Him, which is we must be rooted in the Word of God, and He will build us and establish us, and the devil will not be able to steal because your heart is now the good ground that will produce the thirtyfold, sixty, and a hundredfold.

Final Thought

There is really no secret that we must keep to ourselves when it comes to Jesus Christ. The more we talk about Him, the better off we will be. We have to believe and know that everything that Christ went through was not for His own self but for us. We must believe this in order for us to have faith in Jesus Christ, who is our faith. He was the Word of God-made flesh. He came to show us that everything that the Father has said, He will do that; it can and will be done once we believe. When you read the Gospels, which means the good news, you will notice that there are times when Jesus tells the people that it is not Him that did the healing; it was their own faith. Our own faith will bring us our healing and every other thing that God has promised He will do. Get it established in your heart through His Word that the majority of the things that we want have already been given to us through Christ Jesus, we just have to receive them, and the way God works is that for you to receive anything from Him, you must first believe. Think about this: when you got saved, you did not have to wait a week, and then the Holy Spirit shook you up on the inside and said, "Hello, I am here, living inside of you now." No, it does not work that way. God promised it, and He already sent the Holy Spirit accordingly to the day of Pentecost in the book of Acts chapter 2. This means it is already done. The Holy Spirit is just waiting for you to believe, and He will come into you and dwell within you that same moment that you believe in your heart and confess with your mouth. Confession has a big part to play. We will find out later the importance of confession. Romans chapter 10 tells us how to be saved. You must believe, then confess. In Mark chapter 11 in order for us to receive from God, we must first believe and then speak, aka confess. Confessing is simply acknowledging something you know to be true, and that is the Word of God. Some of us have to renew our minds to be able to understand this, and we can only do that by getting the Word into our hearts. So many people are stuck waiting to receive their healing from God, and God is saying, "I have already done that. I did that when my son, Jesus, was on the cross. Look, don't you see all of His stripes that represent your healing? I have already provided your healing: you must believe and receive."

Chapter 5

FORMULA YES, FORMULA NO

There Must Be a Formula

Before I even thought about writing this book, my goal for myself and other people was to come up with the simplest way to live by faith to learn for myself and to be able to teach other people how to live by faith. I mean, I wanted something that would take you from beginning to end, from start to finish. I was saying to myself and to our heavenly Father. I was talking to myself as if God does not know everything and that I knew what mankind needed. I was saying things like, "I know, God, what we need, and that is a formula." I thought to myself, *Formulas are good, especially in math.* They help in math when they are easy to follow, so a formula for faith should help us to live by faith. This could really be the missing key if a simple formula could be designed. Then, one day God gave me seven nuggets to help inherit the promises of God. I believe, and I have witnessed firsthand, that by doing these seven things, they will help us to see the promises of God manifest in our life. After I received these seven nuggets or seven steps, I was thinking, *Here we go, God is giving me a step-by-step formula.* I thought we are about to change the game with this one. I was thinking that with this formula, people would start walking in victory, no matter what comes their way. So after I received these seven nuggets, I waited, and I waited for more, and there was no more. I waited and waited, and still nothing. Then, one day God spoke to me and said there would be no more. I was like, *What! God, there has to be more; we need help here; what we need is a formula.* Then God said faith is not a formula.

God said, "These nuggets that I have given to you were given in order to help you and other people begin to walk. They were given because too many of my people are stuck standing in the same place, they have given up, and some have even lain down to die. Some have started to run in the wrong direction, chasing after their own lusts and the cares of the world. These things, along with fear, disbelief, and doubt, are drawing them further and further away from Me."

"But each one is tempted when he is drawn away
by his own desires and enticed" (James 1:14).

God said, "I need my people to just start walking. Walk by faith, looking towards the promises in my word. I will bring the promise to you. I will put it before your eyes." When we first find the promise of God for our situation, the way for us to walk may not appear to be clear, you may not even see your pathway at all, but you must begin to walk by faith, trusting and believing in God every step of the way. You must believe that as you begin to walk that you are taking steps that will put you closer to the promise of God in your situation, and as you do, your path will start to appear. This is what is known as stepping out on faith. Remember, Abraham left, not knowing where he was going. He obeyed God, and he was given a path to travel. Remember, Jesus is the way, so keep your eyes on Him, for He is the Word of God. Even when you think you can see Him, continue your walk in faith, listening for direction from the Holy Spirit.

> "Your ears shall hear a word behind you, saying,
> 'This is the way, walk in it,' Whenever you turn
> to the right hand or whenever you turn to the left"
> (Isaiah 30:21).

I don't want to confuse anyone when I say walk. To walk in the Bible is to live. This is how we must live day to day. Looking at His Word, praying, and staying alert to any type of promptings on what to do next, this is how we live, aka how we walk. In order to know which way to go, you must first get to where your path begins, and you can only do that by taking one faith step at a time. Step after step causes you to begin your walk of faith. This allows you to trust that God will reveal your path and supply all of your needs in order for you to be successful on this path.

> "And my God shall supply all your need according to His riches in glory by Christ Jesus" (Philippians 4:19).

But Why No Formula

Even though these seven nuggets or seven steps have been provided, I would still say that they are still not a formula. See, when we take a step, we are looking to see if we have made it there yet or do we need to take another step. As we step, if we begin to see signs of things turning around in our situation, we may stop walking. Now, we are looking for the next sign, and we have ceased to walk by faith, and we have gone back to walking by sight. God said, "If it was a formula, then you would only walk because you are looking for a sign, the next step, and that is not walking by faith; you are walking based on the next sign, and that will turn it into walking by sight and not by faith." These steps were given to keep us walking by faith when there are no signs; therefore, we have to trust God every step of the way. When we take the first step and don't see a change, we have to be willing to take the next step of faith. We do this not knowing what will happen next; whether we will see a change or not, we must know that God is working behind the scenes on our behalf, and then we will not only be walking by faith, but we have begun to live by faith as well. I am not saying that you have to complete all seven steps in order to receive our promise from God because that would be a formula. Some people receive from God as soon as they hear the Word because they simply believed.

And in Lystra a certain man without strength in

his feet was sitting, a cripple from his mother's womb, who had never walked. This man heard Paul speaking. Paul observing him intently and seeing that he had faith to be healed, said with a loud voice, "Stand up straight on your feet!" And he leaped and walked.

Acts 14:8-10

See, God can act whenever and however He wants. Our timetable is not the same as His. So when we think, we should see the promise may not be in line with His time, so we must continue to walk by faith until we get to that time. We can take step after step after step and never see a change; then, the next step we receive from God. You just never know. That is why we cannot stop walking by faith. You may take all seven of the steps in this book and still not receive your promise, but you must know that it is coming, and more will be revealed. Each of our paths is different, causing us to walk accordingly to our path. Therefore, there cannot be a formula because every path is different: some short, some long, some uphill, some downhill. Some paths may even require you to take four steps, then stand still for a while and wait on Him.

"Be still, and know that I am God; I will be exalted among the nations, I will be exalted in the earth!" (Psalm 46:10)

Sometimes, we may have to wait and let the Lord go before us and clear the rest of our path to make our crooked places straight and or to defeat our enemy.

"For this is he who was spoken of by the prophet Isaiah, saying: 'The voice of one crying in the wilderness: Prepare the way of the LORD; Make His paths straight'" (Matthew 3:3).

If God would make the way straight and clear for His son, Jesus, He will do the same for you and me. Remember, we are His sons and daughters too. When you know Him and who you are in Jesus, then it becomes a lot easier to live by faith. He will defeat our enemies. He did it for His chosen people, and we are His chosen children. So why wouldn't He do it for us?

You will not *need* to fight in this *battle*. Position yourselves, stand still and see the salvation of the LORD, who is with you, O Judah and Jerusalem! Do not fear or be dismayed; tomorrow go out against them, for the LORD *is* with you.

2 Chronicles 20:17

"Now when they began to sing and to praise, the LORD set ambushes against the people of Ammon, Moab, and Mount Seir, who had come against Judah; and they were defeated" (2 Chronicles 20:22).

In this story, there are two important things to take away from their victory. One was that they had to stand still and wait on the *Lord*. The next one was that they praised God, and when they praised God, it brought Him on the scene. This is why praise is so important, and we will talk about it later on in this book. So remember, no formula was given; therefore, no formula is needed because if it was needed, it would have been provided. Remember Philippians 4:19, "And my God shall supply all your need according to His riches in glory by Christ Jesus" (Philippians 4:19).

Continue walking by faith and listen for the promptings of the Holy Spirit and focus on the relationship with God as you walk with Him, for He will never leave you nor forsake you.

> "*Let your* conduct *be* without covetousness; *be* content with such things as you have. For He Himself has said, 'I will never leave you nor forsake you'" (Hebrews 13:5).

The reason for this walk may be for that one reason alone, and that is for you to know Him and be close to Him. The reason why I said to focus on Him while you walk by faith is because of Isaiah 26:3.

> "You will keep *him* in perfect peace, *Whose* mind *is* stayed on You, Because he trusts in You" (Isaiah 26:3).

The reason I said your walk might be because God wants to build a relationship with you is that it just may very be based on the same reason why God brought the children of Israel to the wilderness. It was not to punish them; it was for them to get to know their God, their Savior, the One who delivered them out of Egypt.

> And Moses went up to God, and the LORD called to him from the mountain, saying, "Thus you shall say to the house of Jacob, and tell the children of Israel: 'You have seen what I did to the Egyptians, and how I bore you on eagles' wings and brought you to Myself. Now therefore, if you will indeed obey My voice and keep My covenant, then you shall be a special treasure to Me above all people; for all the earth is Mind. And you shall be to Me a kingdom of priests and a holy nation.' These are the words which you shall speak to the children of Israel."

Exodus 19:3-6

God said that He brought the children of Israel to Himself. You may be in a wilderness yourself, and you may be thinking it is an attack from the enemy or a result of the sin in your life, but it may only be that God wants to heal you, He wants to deliver you from the sin that easily traps you, and He can only do that if you get to know Him. Remember, Jesus could not do a lot of miracles in His own town because they thought they knew Him. Ask yourself this question, "Am I the reason that God cannot work in my life because I think I know Him when I really don't?" It could be as simple as spending time in your Bible with Him, praying more, and you could be walking out of your situation in victory because you now know who your Father is, and you will know He brought you to the wilderness that you may know Him.

Final Thought

To know all of these truths that are within God's Word will do you no good. You have to believe them with your heart. The only way you will be able to believe with your heart, the way the Bible is talking about begins with you and the effort you put into establishing your heart. You will have to give time to the word. Giving time to the Word is not just glancing at it for a minute or two; you have to really pay attention to what you are reading. Next, you have to say the Word because we know that faith comes by hearing and hearing the Word of God. Also, when you say the Word and agree with the word, then you start confessing the word. Now, you have taken it to a new level of just saying it; now, you are talking about it to others, and you have begun to confess the word. Every time you do this, you are putting the Word into your heart. The Bible tells us to let the Word of Christ dwell in us richly. We already know that nothing can come out of you if it is not already in you, so we must get the Word in us and keep feeding on the Word so that is all that will come out of us. When I say that the Word is the only thing that will come out of us, I mean what we say, how we act, and how we react, and this is how Jesus lived, and the Word will transform our lives that we will live just like Jesus did. Add more words daily to what you already have and continue adding more words, and as you begin to feed off of the word, then you will see that you will start becoming what you are saying, what you are confessing, and this helps build your character. Then you begin to believe everything that is in God's Word because you are seeing it firsthand now. You are looking for it in every situation, and when you begin to do this, that means you are looking for Him first in everything that happens, whether in your life or the life of someone around you who is close to you. Whether the situation is good or bad, you will be looking for Him. It has become your nature to look for Him in everything, and that is where we need to be in life in order for us to walk in continuous victory. When this happens, you will notice that God has been there the entire time, and now that you have His Word established in your heart, you have given Him something to work with and let me tell you, our heavenly Father loves to work on our behalf. A lot of times, I have asked God to show me things in the Bible, and He just starts to show out. It is almost like He has taken over my entire body, and I can turn the page to the exact page that I need to be on, and my eyes will travel to the exact spot where my answer is. Then, I will do this nine or ten more times and will have the same result every time. While I am doing this, it feels like I am on fire on the inside. I can't explain it, but I know that His presence is heavy on me, and so I take advantage of that time, lol. I will ask Him all kinds of stuff, and He is allowed to work in my life because I have given Him something to work with. My faith is me believing that if I continue to feed on His Word and establish my heart, then He will come and perform everything that He said He would, and this allows me to have God's best for me in my life.

Chapter 6

SEVEN STEPS MIXED WITH PRAISE, WORSHIP, AND LOVE

The Steps

We have come to the part of the book that I know you, as the reader, have been waiting for. The seven steps are important, but the first five chapters are just important. Without having the knowledge that is provided within the first five chapters, the seven steps would not be of any use to you, nor would the rest of the book really be any good to you. They all go together, just like shoes. One shoe would not be any good to you because you have two feet, and shoes come as a pair. So is it with all of the information that is provided within this book? It is all needed and must be used together, so here we go. I will not keep you waiting any longer. The first step is to find your promise and make your request known. Remember, each step has its own chapter, and I will go more into detail with each step in its own chapter. Next is to keep your eyes on your promise. Next is to hear your promise over and over and over. Then mediate on your promise until you are full. Next is for us to give thanks continuously.

Then, you must pray for others, specifically for those that you know who are going through exactly what you are going through. Then, you must pray in the Spirit. This is needed because even though what we are going through is what we are asking, deliverance from it may only be a symptom and not the root cause. The Holy Spirit knows all things; He knows the perfect will of God in your life, so He will pray in line that which will attack the root cause. Also, by praying in the Spirit, we will build ourselves up on our most holy faith.

Praise and Worship

Outside of getting to know who God is through prayer and spending time in His Word, the next important thing is to praise and worship Him. We know that we were created to fellowship with Him and that we were created to praise Him. Psalm 145 and Psalm 150 verse 6 are a great place for us to start. It tells us that the Lord is gracious and full of compassion, that He is good to all, and that His tender mercies are over all His works, and lastly, that all of His works shall praise Him.

The LORD *is* gracious and full of compassion, Slow to anger and great in mercy. The LORD *is* good to all, And His tender mercies *are* over all His works. All Your works shall praise You, O LORD, And Your saints shall bless You.

Psalm 145:8-10

72

"Let everything that has breath praise the LORD. Praise the LORD!" (Psalm 150:6)

Now, the Word "works" here in these verses also means His creations. He created us so we fit into that category of "all His works," so that means we shall praise Him. "Shall" means it will happen, so we need to make it part of our lifestyle and not as a ritual. Psalm 150:6 makes it even clearer. It states that everything that has breath, which includes you and me, will praise God. In one of the Student Bible Dictionaries I had, "praise" means to adore God for who he is and that it is a form of prayer as well. It also means to express honor and gratitude to God through worship, words, attitudes, and actions.

See, when we adore God and give Him His proper honor, respect, and recognition, then we are truly praising God. As a plus to all of that, the fear of the *Lord* is the same exact thing. For "fear" means reverence, respect, and it is a realization of holiness, not in terror but in honor and recognition of position. Proverbs 1:7 tells us that the fear of the *Lord* is the beginning of knowledge.

"The fear of the LORD *is* the beginning of knowledge, *But* fools despise wisdom and instruction" (Proverbs 1:7).

Remember, we must know Him, so praising has to be a part of our lifestyle if we want to continuously walk in victory. Now, "worship" means to adore, obey, reverence, focus positive attention, and enjoy the presence of God. It can be any action or attitude that expresses praise, love, and appreciation for God. What I want to focus on is the "to enjoy" and the "presence of God" part of this definition. Psalm 16:11 tells us that in the presence of God is the fullness of joy, and at His right hand are pleasures forevermore.

"You will show me the path of life; In Your presence *is* fullness of joy; At Your right hand *are* pleasures forevermore" (Psalm 16:11).

The reason why I want to focus on these two parts is that they go together. You can't have the fullness of joy and all of His pleasures outside of His presence. So, let's explore what it means to be in His presence.

Praise to Enter His Presence

We see that in His presence is the fullness of joy. I don't think too many people like being sad and mad all the time. Notice, I didn't say everyone because I know a few that love to live their lives like that, and I hurt for them because that is not how our heavenly Father wants us to live. Remember, I told you that God supplies all of our needs, and if we needed it, He would give it to us. Well, we need joy in order to live in this dying world, and He gave us joy when we accepted Jesus Christ as our Lord and Savior. When we did this, we became a new creation with the Holy Spirit living within us, and with Him came fruits, and one of those fruits is joy.

"Therefore, if anyone is in Christ, he is a new creation; old things have passed away; behold, all things have become new" (2 Corinthians 5:17).

"But the fruit of the Spirit is love, joy, peace, long-suffering, kindness, goodness, faithfulness, gentleness, self-control. Against such there is no law" (Galatians 5:22-23).

So we now know that joy is within us. You may be thinking, *Well, if we have joy in us, what do we need praise for?* The Holy Spirit is a well of water within us. A well is full of water, but unless you go to the well and draw water from it, you will not have anything to drink. So, we must draw from the well, the Holy Spirit, who is the Spirit of God Himself, and we must go to Him by entering into His presence, and to enter into His presence, we must praise and worship. Remember, worship is an action or attitude that expresses praise, love, and appreciation for God. Psalm 95:1-2 tells us before we enter His presence, for us to sing, shout, and give thanks.

"Oh come, let us sing to the LORD! Let us shout joyfully to the Rock of our salvation. Let us come before His presence with thanksgiving; Let us shout joyfully to Him with psalms" (Psalm 95:1-2).

Psalm 100 tells us that we come before His presence with joyful shouts, gladness, singing, giving thanks, with praise and blessings on His name.

> Make a joyful shout to the LORD, all you lands! Serve the LORD with gladness; Come before His presence with singing. Know that the LORD, He is God; It is He who has made us, and not we ourselves; We are His people and the sheep of His pasture. Enter into His gates with thanksgiving, And into His courts with praise. Be thankful to Him, and bless His name. For the LORD is good; His mercy is everlasting, And His truth endures to all generations.

Psalm 100

Now we know why praise and worship are so important because it brings us before His presence, and we know in His presence is the fullness of joy and all of His pleasures.

Praise Brings Him on the Scene

Now I know that I have been through something in my life that I had to go through alone, and I wished that I could have had someone there with me to help me go through. Well, God said that He would never leave us nor forsake us. So when I go through now, I ask Him to pull up with me or to pull up on me; lol! I do this by praising because praising brings God on the scene. We first see this truth in 2 Chronicles 5:11-14.

> And it came to pass when the priests came out
> of the Most Holy Place (for all the priests who
> were present had sanctified themselves, without
> keeping to their divisions), and the Levites who
> were the singers, all those of Asaph and Heman
> and Jeduthun, with their sons and their brethren,
> stood at the east end of the altar, clothed in white
> linen, having cymbals, stringed instruments and
> harps, and with them one hundred and twenty
> priests sounding with trumpets—indeed it came
> to pass, when the trumpeters and singers were as
> one, to make one sound to be heard in praising
> and thanking the LORD, and when they lifted up
> their voice with the trumpets and cymbals and in-
> struments of music, and praised the LORD, saying:
> "For He is good, For His mercy endures forever,"
> that the house, the house of the LORD, was filled
> with a cloud, so that the priests could not continue
> ministering because of the cloud; for the glory of
> the LORD filled the house of God.

2 Chronicles 5:11-14

Notice that they were singing, playing different instruments, that they were praising and giving thanks, then all of a sudden God showed up. It says that the glory of the *Lord* filled the entire house. Now, let's look at another example. In 2 Chronicles 20:21-22, we witness again that the people were singing and praising, and as they did, the *Lord* showed up and defeated their enemies for them.

> And when he had consulted with the people, he appointed those who should sing to the LORD, and who should praise the beauty of holiness, as they went out before the army and were saying: "Praise the LORD, For His mercy endures forever." Now when they began to sing and to praise, the LORD set ambushes against the people of Ammon, Moab, and Mount Seir, who had come against Judah; and they were defeated.

2 Chronicles 20:21-22

My last example is 2 Kings 3:15.

> "But now bring me a musician. Then it happened, when the musician played, that the hand of the LORD came upon him" (2 Kings 3:15).

We see here that Elisha asked for someone to come and play music. When the musician began to play, the spirit of God came upon Elisha. It is clear when we want God on the scene or when we want to enter into His presence, and we must praise and worship. Psalm 22:3 tells us that God is enthroned in the praises of Israel.

"But You are holy, Enthroned in the praises of Israel" (Psalm 22:3).

The King James Version says He inhabits our praise. Webster's dictionary defines "inhabit" as to live in. This is just another example that shows us that when we need to enter into His presence when the storm that surrounds us is so dark, our heavenly Father can be found when we praise and worship Him, and that is when we find out that He has been right there in the midst of it all with us the entire time. So start singing, dancing, shouting, and giving thanks because of who our heavenly Father is, what He wants to do for us now, and all the things that He has already done for us, those known and unknown.

Love

We have to operate in love, not in the world's love but in God's love. One of the main keys to God's love, which is known as *agape* love, is to forgive. We must forgive everybody. Faith wants work without love, and love is not present when unforgiveness is still on the scene. Paul told us in the book of Galatians that faith will only work by love.

"For in Christ Jesus neither circumcision nor uncircumcision avails anything, but faith working through love" (Galatians 5:6).

This is why Jesus, after He taught His disciples how to pray, He instructed them to forgive.

> "For if you forgive men their trespasses, your heavenly Father will also forgive you. But if you do not forgive men their trespasses, neither will your Father forgive your trespasses" (Matthew 6:14-15).

We want God to forgive us of our wrongs so that we can receive from Him, but Jesus is saying, "If you don't forgive your brother, then God will not forgive you, and you will not be able to receive from God." If we are not operating out of love, then our faith has no power to draw from. Jesus backs this up again in Mark 11:22-26.

> So Jesus answered and said to them, "Have faith in God. For assuredly, I say to you, whoever says to this mountain, 'Be removed and be cast into the sea,' and does not doubt in his heart, but believes that those things he says will be done, he will have whatever he says. Therefore I say to you, whatever things you ask when you pray, believe that you receive them, and you will have them.

> "And whenever you stand praying, if you have anything against anyone, forgive him, that your Father in heaven may also forgive you your trespasses. But if you do not forgive, neither will your

Father in heaven forgive your trespasses."

Mark 11:22-26

When you pray and ask God for something, you must forgive in order for your faith to work so that you can receive it. The type of love, agape love, is the type of love that God is talking about, is found in 1 Corinthians 13:4-8. Before we get into these verses, I want to explain what I mean about the Word love and how it is used in the Bible. In the Greek language, there are several different types of love that have different meanings. They have a word for love that deals with loving your brother, your relatives, a sexual love, and then the God kind of love. For us, in the English language, we just have the word love. In the Bible, you can see the Word love, but you would have to know what Greek word was used there because it could have three to four different meanings, and we are trying to apply it to the only meaning of love that we have in the English language. An example of what I am saying is you can see the Word "love," and you are trying to apply it to a brotherly love that you have with your family and friends, but the way it was used in the Greek form is an erotic type of love, so you would be trying to use this love in a wrong way. So in order for us to be able to forgive and live, how Jesus taught us to live is to live in agape love, which means God's kind of love. This is the same love that Jesus was talking about when He said, "Love your enemy," and this is the same type of love that Paul is talking about here in 1 Corinthians 13.

Love suffers long and is kind; love does not envy; love does not parade itself, is not puffed up; does not behave rudely, does not seek its own, is not provoked, thinks no evil; does not rejoice in iniquity, but rejoices in the truth; bears all things, believes all things, hopes all things, endures all things. Love never fails. But whether there are prophecies, they will fail; whether there are tongues, they will cease; whether there is knowledge, it will vanish away.

1 Corinthians 13:4-8

We must operate in this type of love because verse 8 tells us agape never fails. You will never fail if you operate in this type of love. Then in verses 4 through 8, where the Word "love" is, I want you to put your name there and begin to confess that you suffer long that you are kind. That you do not envy and that you never give up. You care more for others than you do for yourself. You don't want what you don't have and that you don't strut. You don't have the big head and that you don't force yourself on others, and you don't have the mindset of me first. You don't fly off the handle, and you don't keep a list of all the sins of others, nor do you remember, nor do you hold on to how many times people have done you wrong. You don't celebrate when others beg, and you take pleasure in the blossoming of truth. You put up with anything, and you trust God always. You always look for the best, and you never look back. Lastly, you keep going to the end. Now ask yourself, "Have I been walking in agape love?" If you have not, then it is necessary that you do in order for you to have the life that Jesus had here on earth. The more you confess this, the easier it will become for you to do. So go ahead and start walking in love because your faith is operating from your source of love.

Final Thought

We are about to get into the seven steps or seven nuggets, but they won't do us any good if we are not praising and worshipping God. These are the things that we were created to do. If we want God to do His part, then we must also do our part. Our part is more than just having faith, we must obey, and part of obeying is praising and worshipping God along with walking in love. These nuggets will really teach us how to live by faith. Praise and worship put us where we need to be in this world. It puts us right next to God. Think about Adam and Eve. They were in His presence, and they lacked nothing. They were deceived because they thought that they were missing out on something. Don't be deceived like they were. I promise you that you will not be missing out on anything when you take away time from yourself and the world to praise and worship God. God supplies all of our needs, and He gives us richly all things to enjoy. So how can you miss out on anything? It is not like we have the power to go out and get it ourselves. We must understand our dependency on God like a newborn baby needs his parents. The baby depends on his parents to feed him, to give him a bath, to carry him from place to place, to help him burp, and this is something that the body does on its own, but for a newborn, it is helpless, yet at the same time, it is provided with everything it needs.

There are things that we can do ourselves, but we need God to help us with it, or we will end up in a lot of pain. The same way a newborn feels when he needs to burp. Like the newborn baby, we must become the same way with God. We must stop doing so much and start depending on Him more, and as you stop the doing and let God work, you can spend the time that you would have wasted doing it yourself and use that time now to praise and worship God. If we truly love God like we say we do, then this has to be a must in our lives, both in the good times as well as in the bad times. As we are praising Him, remember His commandment of love, agape love. Look at every person you come across as your potential brother or sister in Christ. Supply any need that they may have without looking for anything in return. Most of us are already like that with our blood brothers and sisters. Some of us are like that with our closest friends, but Jesus has commanded us to take it a step further and to extend this same love to each other, to the stranger, to the fatherless, to the widow. Let's praise God and love Him and love one another and witness and experience the true presence of God in our life.

Chapter 7

FIND YOUR PROMISE AND MAKE YOUR REQUEST KNOWN

Finding Your Promise

It is important to find your promise. See, we know that God cannot lie, so if God said something about a particular situation, then it has to be true. Regardless of what we see and what we have heard, God's Words have the final say, so and that is how it is going to be. Yes, what we see and hear are the facts at that particular time. What I want you to know is that facts can change, but the truth never changes. God's Words are true, and God is His Word. And we know that He never changes and that He remains the same.

"In the beginning was the Word, and the Word was with God, and the Word was God" (John 1:1).

"And the Word became flesh and dwelt among us, and we beheld His glory, the glory as of the only begotten of the Father, full of grace and truth" (John 1:14).

"Jesus Christ is the same yesterday, today, and forever" (Hebrews 13:8).

God said in His Word that He would give us the victory over whatever we are facing. The victory will be given to us through our Lord Jesus Christ.

"But thanks *be* to God, who gives us the victory through our Lord Jesus Christ" (1 Corinthians 15:57).

Also, in His Word, it tells us that we are more than conquerors through Him, who loves us, and that Jesus always leads us in triumph.

"Yet in all these things we are more than conquerors through Him who loved us" (Romans 8:37).

"Now thanks *be* to God who always leads us in triumph in Christ, and through us diffuses the fragrance of His knowledge in every place" (2 Corinthians 2:14).

His Word also tells us that we can overcome the world.

"For whatever is born of God overcomes the world. And this is the victory that has overcome the world-our faith" (1 John 5:4).

Now you may be saying, "Okay, those are just generic

promises that do not talk about what I am going through." Well, this is how it works. If you are sick, God gives us the victory to overcome that sickness. You can gain the victory over that sickness; you can conquer that sickness when you find out what His promise is for sickness. First Peter 2:24 tells us that the work is already done through Jesus, and by His stripes, you are already healed. You just have to receive it, and that is where faith comes in.

> "Who Himself bore our sins in His own body on the tree, that we, having died to sins, might live for righteousness—by whose stripes you were healed" (1 Peter 2:24).

To get anything from God, you must receive it by faith. If I send you money through money gram, even if I give you the information, you still have to have faith that it will be there when you go to pick it up—or you will never go and get it. Everything we are asking God, for He has already given it to us freely through Jesus. We just have to receive it.

Now you may be asking, "If it is mine and He has given it to me, then why do I have to ask?" The answer is simple because Jesu told us to.

> "Therefore do not be like them. For your Father knows the things you have need of before you ask Him" (Matthew 6:8).

"Ask, and it will be given to you; seek, and you will find; knock, and it will be opened to you" (Matthew 7:7).

And in that day you will ask Me nothing. Most assuredly, I say to you, whatever you ask the Father in My name He will give you. Until now you have asked nothing in My name. Ask, and you will receive, that your joy may be full.

John 16:23-24

Even James tells us we have not received from God because we have not asked or we asked for the wrong reason.

You lust and do not have, You murder and covet and cannot obtain. You fight and war. Yet you do not have because you do not ask. You ask and do not receive, because you ask amiss, that you may spend it on your pleasures.

James 4:2-3

Notice, the title of this chapter is to find your promise first, then ask God for it by letting your request be known. Have you ever had an elderly relative or friend that would give you anything you wanted regardless of how often you asked them for something? Now on the flip side, came one thing with this person. They always required you to come and sit with them, talk with them, and spend time with them.

Well, it is the same way with your heavenly Father. He loves you and wants to bless you, but He also wants to spend time with you, and that is why we ask for things in prayer. That is when He gets to spend time with us. For those of you who are married and have older kids, you love phone calls, text messages, emails, and even face time, but nothing compares to that one on one time of being in each other's presence. Well, that is what the *Lord* wants. Where do you think you got it from? Remember, we are created in His likeness and in His image. Trust me; once you have truly entered into His presence, you will try to stay there because there is no other feeling in the world that compares to it. Everyone's experience is different, but I will do my best to describe my own. When I am in the presence of the *Lord,* there is something that comes over my entire body, a feeling that I don't know how to explain. And when I am in His presence, if I was hungry before, I am not even hungry while I am with Him; I don't even know that I was hungry, and everything that was troubling me is gone; I don't even know it exists. All I know is to focus on Him. I promise you it will change your life.

Okay, now back to finding your promise. This can be done with a concordance. Some Bibles have them in the back, or you can purchase a concordance that is full of God's Word and where you can find it in the Bible. One of the Bibles I have not only has a concordance in the back, but it also has a section titled "Key Bible Promises." For example, if I need strength, it will give me places to turn to in the Bible, so I can find out what God promised to me when it comes to the situation that I am currently going through. An example of this would be if I needed strength, then there is a list of verses that I could pray about and make them my own so that I can receive strength. With the technology we have, this can also be done through almost any search engine on the web. Remember, knowing is half the battle; now, get in there and find your promises from God and move on to the second part of this step.

Making Your Request Known

Some of you may be saying, "I don't know how to pray." Don't freak out just yet because the Bible tells us that even when people groan in the Bible, it is a form of prayer (notice, I said groaning and not complaining, for the Bible tells us not to complain).

"Do all things without complaining and disputing" (Philippians 2:14).

Notice in John chapter 11 when Jesus went to where Lazarus had died. When you look at verse 33, then verses 41 and 42, they will shed some light on what I am saying. In verse 33, it tells us that Jesus groaned from within. Then in verses 41 and 42, it tells us that when He spoke to our heavenly Father, he said, "I know that you heard me when I prayed." Nowhere in chapter 11 does it tell us that he prayed except for verse 33 when he groaned. I will give you some other examples to put a stamp on it, so you will feel better about praying to your heavenly Father.

> "Therefore, when Jesus saw her weeping, and the Jews who came with her weeping, He groaned in the spirit and was troubled" (John 11:33).

> Then they took away the stone from the place where the dead man was lying. And Jesus lifted up His eyes and said, "Father I thank You that You have heard Me. And I know that You always hear Me, but because of the people who are standing by I said this, that they may believe that You sent me."

> **John 11:41-42**

In Exodus chapters two and three, we see here that God talks about hearing the children of Israel cry and groan, and He has come to answer their prayers.

> Now it happened in the process of time that the king of Egypt died. Then the children of Israel groaned because of the bondage, and they cried out; and their cry came up to God because of the bondage. So God heard their groaning, and God remembered His covenant with Abraham, with Isaac, and with Jacob. And God looked upon the children of Israel, and God acknowledged them.

> **Exodus 2:23-25**

"And the LORD said, "I have surely seen the oppression of My people who are in Egypt, and have heard their cry because of their taskmasters, for I know their sorrows" (Exodus 3:7).

"Now therefore, behold, the cry of the children of Israel has come to Me, and I have also seen the oppression with which the Egyptians oppress them" (Exodus 3:9).

Another example of prayer can be found in 1 Samuel chapter one. Here we see Samuel's mother crying. She does not even speak a word. Eli notices her lips moving, but no sound is coming out. Have you ever been so beat down, so broken, so at the end of your road that you couldn't get any words out and all you could do is cry? Well, cheer up because God heard you, and He saw your tears just like He saw Hannah's tears.

So Hannah arose after they had finished eating and drinking in Shiloh. Now Eli the priest was sitting on the seat by the doorpost of the tabernacle of the LORD. And she was in bitterness of soul, and prayed to the LORD and wept in anguish. Then she made a vow and said "O LORD of hosts, if You will indeed look on the affliction of Your maidservant and remember me, and not forget Your maidservant, but will give Your maidservant a male child, then I will give him to the LORD all the days of his life, and no razor shall come upon his head." And it happened, as she continued praying before the LORD, that Eli watched her mouth. Now Hannah spoke in her heart; only her lips moved, but her voice was not heard. Therefore Eli thought she was drunk.

1 Samuel 1:9-13

Prayer is simply talking to God. It is simply spending time with Him as you would with a family member or friend. Refer to the book of Psalm and notice how David talked to God. Notice how he told God about the things he was going through and that they were not right and how they made him feel, and then he would thank God. He would cheer himself up because he knew God heard him, and he knew God loved him enough that he would not let his enemies overpower him. Now, if David can have that type of confidence with God, we must get to that same level with God in our relationship. Also, David did not have the written word of God as we do, so we need to be more confident because we are praying His will, what He says about our situation, plus we are sons of God; remember, David was just His servant.

Besides groaning, we see that people have shared tears as well, and they were considered a form of prayer. What we will focus on is praying the perfect will of God into your situation. I want you to have the confidence that the apostle John was talking about so that you can really rest and rejoice because you know that God has heard you and that you will have what you asked for in Jesus' name. Let me explain this first. God's will is His Word, so if you ask accordingly to His Word, according to what He has said about your situation, then we will have the confidence that what we have asked for we will receive because it is His will.

> Now this is the confidence that we have in Him, that if we ask anything according to His will, He hears us. And if we know that He hears us, whatever we ask, we know that we have the petitions that we have asked of Him.

1 John 5:14-15

Don't let people trip you up because of their lack of knowledge of who our Father is. They will tell you, "Well, if it is God's will, you don't know what God is going to do." Well, I have shown you the things that He delights in, and I have shown you that His Words, aka His will, do not come back to Him void. What those people should be saying is that God will is about to happen in your life when you start living by faith, and we know exactly what He is going to do because He has given us His Word; we just don't know how He is going to get it done because His ways are not our ways and His thoughts are not our thoughts. When it comes to His will, we know because He has given it to us through His Word and remember it is impossible for God to lie.

Prayer Allows Us to Rest

Here is another reason for prayer, and that is to allow us to rest. If you could do anything to get rid of or help your situation, then it would have already been done. Since we can't do it, we are at the point where we are still stuck. It still exists, and we can't rest until something is done about it or something is done that we have confidence in that we can rest that things are moving and working for our good. If we know that someone is doing the work for us, then we can rest because we believe that it is being handled. Well, that is what it means for us to labor to enter into God's rest. He is not asking us to do the work because the work has already been done. The only work that is required is for us to renew our minds so that we can believe. If we can believe, then we can rest because we know that God will take care of the situation because He said He would.

So, pray God's will in your life and rest knowing everything is taking care of by Him, our heavenly Father, and that is why we can rejoice and give thanks to because all we had to do is pray and believe, and God did the rest.

"Then they said to Him, "What shall we do, that we may work the works of God?" Jesus answered and said to them, "This is the work of God, that you believe in Him whom He sent" (John 6:28-29).

"For we who have believed do enter that rest, as He has said, "So I swore in My wrath, They shall not enter My rest," although the works were finished from the foundation of the world" (Hebrews 4:3).

Here is the good news. When we face a problem, we find our promise, ask God to help us accordingly to His will, His Word, then give thanks, rejoice every day, and rest. We do this because we know Him, we have a relationship with Him, and we know He will do what He says and that He will give us the desires of our heart. We can now rest because we know that He can, and He will give us the victory accordingly to His Word through Jesus Christ. Remember, His Word does not come back to Him void, and He cannot lie. Also, we must know that He works all things out for the good of those who love Him. Now, ask yourself: do you love him, do you believe that you have been chosen?

"And we know that all things work together for good to those who love God, to those who are the called according to His purpose" (Romans 8:28).

An Example Prayer

Here is an example of how I would use God's Word to help from my prayer. Let's say I lacked wisdom in a certain situation that I was facing or about to face. First, I would ask my heavenly Father to forgive me of the sins I had committed, those knowingly and those unknown. For the sin that I do know about, I have to bring them before God. I will have to bring them before Him if I want to be forgiven, plus our heavenly Father already knows where I have fallen short, so why try and hide it. By doing this, it helps to build the relationship with Him, and it keeps you close to God because when we live in sin, it separates us from God. Then I would remind God of His Word that in James 1:5 said to you that if a man lacks wisdom, then he should ask God, who gives to all liberally and without reproach. So, I'm asking you, dear heavenly Father, for wisdom in my current situation, and I pray that you fill me with the knowledge of your will and all your wisdom and spiritual understanding for my current situation, in Jesus' name. Amen.

> "If any of you lacks wisdom, let him ask of God, who gives to all liberally and without reproach, and it will be given to him" (James 1:5).

> "For this reason we also, since the day we heard it, do not cease to pray for you, and to ask that you may be filled with the knowledge of His will in all wisdom and spiritual understanding" (Colossians 1:9).

Now I have to use faith. Faith is saying that I have the wisdom even though I may not have received it yet. So if I have it, I'm no longer going to ask God for it; I am going to thank Him for it as if I already have it. We will get more into thanksgiving later in this book, but this is the beginning of our faith walk. When we do this, we will have to continue looking at the promise of God, the blueprint of our faith, aka our hope, and this leads us to the topic of the next chapter, "Keep Your Eyes on the Promise."

Final Thought

You must find the promises of God for you within His Word when it comes to your situation. When you find out what God says about your situation, then go to Him in prayer. Let His Word be the final word when it comes to your situation. Believe and be confident that God heard you because you are His righteousness and that we can receive from Him because of who we are to Him in Christ Jesus. Believe that He will answer your prayer; believe that your prayer has already been answered because of what Jesus Christ had already done at the cross over two thousand years ago. You can rest knowing that God has answered your prayer not based on what you can or cannot do or what you have or have not done. He did it because of who you are in Christ and because you acted in faith accordingly to His Word. If we believe, then we can receive. Remember, you don't have to come up with some fancy big words, just speak to Him and let Him know that you believe His Word and that you are making His Word final in your situation. You are letting it be known that you believe His Word over any other word and that you are about to rest because you know you have received what you asked for because you asked accordingly to His will, and you know that He will move mountains if He has to in order to bring forth His promises in your life. God is good, my brothers and sisters, because we have not done anything to deserve His mercy and His love.

Chapter 8

KEEP YOUR EYES ON THE PROMISE

Why Must I Continue to Look at My Promise?

Some of you may be saying if I found my promise and I prayed about it, then why do I have to keep looking at it. We must continue to look at our promise or promises depending on what all you are going through for two reasons. One reason is the Bible tells us to and, secondly, when you have something of value, you have to protect it. To protect it, you will keep watch over it. You will lock it up somewhere where you feel that it is safe. Well, the thing of value that you must keep a watch on and protect is the Word of God. It is like having a lottery ticket worth billions, and you can't cash it in until next week. Would you let that ticket out of your sight? No, I didn't think so; therefore, we must be the same way about God's Word until we can cash in on it, meaning until it is manifested in the natural. We know that the devil is coming to try and steal the word, it is your job to keep this from happening, and the first step is to keep your eye on your lottery ticket, which is the Word of God.

My son, give attention to my words; Incline your

ear to my sayings. Do not let them depart from your eyes; Keep them in the midst of your heart; For they *are* life to those who find them, And health to all their flesh.

Proverbs 4:20-22

This Book of the Law shall not depart from your mouth, but you shall meditate in it day and night, that you may observe to do according to all that is written in it. For then you will make your way prosperous and then you will have good success.

Joshua 1:8

One thing I can tell you is this: if your mom or dad told you that in order for you to get a toy when you went to the store, you had to be good and do what they told you to do. If you did not, then you would not get a toy when they went to the store, correct. Well, I'm telling you that the one thing outside of not believing in God's Word or doubting His Word that will keep you from receiving from God is disobedience. We must obey God and do what His Word tells us to do. The reason why Joshua had success is that he meditated on God's Word day and night. We can be successful just like Joshua was, but we must do the same thing that he did, and that is to keep the words of God before our eyes. This is important. Look at what God told His people in Deuteronomy.

And these words which I command you today

shall be in your heart. You shall teach them diligently to your children, and shall talk of them
when you sit in your house, when you walk by the
way, when you lie down, and when you rise up.
You shall bind them as a sign on your hand, and
they shall be as frontlets between your eyes. You
shall write them on the doorpost of your house
and on your gates.

Deuteronomy 6:6-9

The most important thing we should get from this is that
we must obey God. God is ready to do His part, but it is up to
us to do our part. Our part is to believe in His Word and obey.
You must believe that by following God's commands, we
will be successful like Joshua. I will discuss obeying a little
more in detail later within this chapter, but let's get back on
keeping the Word before our eyes.

So, we see here that God wanted us to continue to stay in
His Word. Why? Well, for starters, His Word gives us light.
It brings light into our entire body. We need light because we
know the enemy we are fighting is the power of darkness.
So in order to weaken him, we must remove all darkness
from within our bodies. Also, ignorance is considered to be
darkness, and God is holding us responsible for our own ignorance. So when we get rid of the ignorance, we get rid of a
hiding place for the devil, and we can take that territory back
which he has stolen.

"The lamp of the body is the eye. If therefore your eye is good, your whole body will be full of light" (Matthew 6:22).

Next, we must continue to remind ourselves of what God has said. See, the enemy will put your problem right in front of you, and that is all that you can focus on, and that is all you will talk about and think about, and this will lead to depression, anxiety, fear, and a host of other things. Well, God wants His Word in front of your eyes so you can think about Him and His Word all day so that you can talk about Him and have good feelings, feelings of joy, love, peace, and righteousness. Are you beginning to see the picture? This is how God's way is, but the devil, not having his own way, takes what God does through His Word and try and have the same effect by bringing forth problems for us to focus on to take our mind off of our heavenly Father and to try and get us to focus on the illusion that the enemy is trying to trick us into accepting.

This is what happened with Peter. We all know the story that Peter walked on water; then, he began to sink. And as he was sinking, he cried out to Jesus, and Jesus saved him by putting him back into the boat, and then the winds ceased. Peter's example is the main reason we must keep the Word of God before our eyes. It is needed because we need to begin to see ourselves as the Bible says we are. It is only when we take our eyes off the Word of God that we begin to fall, and that is what happened to Peter. There are three major things that happen in this story that I want to bring to your attention. First, Peter took a step of faith. If he had used his carnal mind, he would have said, "Wait a minute, I can't walk on water." He did not think at all because he was so focused on Jesus, the Word of God, that when Jesus said to come, he obeyed.

Notice, Peter did not begin to sink until he took his eyes off of Jesus. He started looking at the winds that were around him. Those same winds were there when he first stepped out on the boat, but they were nothing to him until he looked at them. This is true for us as well. We can be having a good day, we have forgotten about our problems, then we either hear something, see something, or think about the wrong thing, then our problems have just become big again, and those thoughts ruin the entire day. Those problems were there earlier, but notice they did not bother you until you gave them some attention. That is why God said, "Keep your eyes on My word, and My word will produce thoughts of Me." And whoever's mind is on Him, and He will give them peace. The last thing I want to point out is that when Peter took his step of faith, where was Christ? He was there every step of the way with him, and when Peter failed, he cried out to Jesus, and Jesus saved him and not only put him back in the boat, but the same storm that had prevented them from making it to the other side, the same storm that caused Peter to take his eyes off of Jesus causing him to almost drown, Jesus caused it to cease. See, when we take this step of faith, we give Jesus enough to work with. And he not only saved Peter but ceased the storm that was giving all of the trouble that day.

> Now in the fourth watch of the night Jesus went to them, walking on the sea. And when the disciples saw Him walking on the sea, they were troubled, saying, "It is a ghost!" And they cried out for fear. But immediately Jesus spoke to them, saying, "Be of good Cheer! It is I; do not be afraid." And Peter answered Him and said, "Lord if it is You, command me to come to You on the water." So He said, "Come." And when Peter had come down out of the boat, he walked on the water to go to Jesus. But when he saw that the wind was boisterous, he was afraid; and beginning to sink he cried out, saying, "Lord, save me!" And immediately Jesus stretched out His hand and caught him, and said to him, "O you of little faith, why did you doubt?" And when they got into the boat, the wind ceased.

Matthew 14:25-32

Another reason why it is needed for us to keep the Word before us is to help us notice when an attack is coming. If you are focused on God's Word, and that is what you are reading and thinking about, then all of a sudden you get a thought about an old boyfriend or girlfriend that you had and the good times the both of you used to have, then the light bulb will come on. You will be able to recognize the attack. If I am focused on God's Word and thinking about His promises, then where in the world did this thought come from. It is an attack from the enemy to get you to take your mind off of God and to lure you away by your own evil desires and lust.

"But each one is tempted when he is drawn away by his own desires and enticed" (James 1:14).

See, one of his tactics is to get your mind off of God and get your mind on something that will cause you to sin or will cause you to fear and begin to doubt that God will really do what He said He would do. That is why we must keep the Word before our eyes. The enemy that is against us does not send a text message that says, "Be ready at 3:30 today; I am coming by to try and knock you off your horse." No, we don't know when he is coming, but it will be easier to identify when he does come if you are focusing on God and His promises for your situation.

Think about this for a moment. Have you ever noticed that when something bad happens, or something goes wrong, or we know something has happened, but we don't know what, how is it so easy for us to automatically think or vision something wrong? I mean, we can envision detail by detail, image by image, and majority of the time the worst has not happened, and the other times what our fear produced did not happen either, but we have worried and caused ourselves to fear, to have depression and anxiety when nothing has happened. Now, if we focus on something long enough, and we are constantly talking about it, we can bring it into reality. Proverbs 18:21 tells us that the power to bring life or death into existence is in the words that we speak from our mouths.

> "Death and life are in the power of the tongue,
> And those who love it will eat its fruit" (Proverbs
> 18:21).

In the same ways that fear causes us to think the worst and causes us to picture bad things happening to us, faith causes us to picture and think the promises of God. When we keep our eyes on God's Word long enough, we will start to think about His promises, and we will begin to develop images of us with God's promises.

Lastly, we protect the Word by keeping it before our eyes. Remember, the enemy's job is to steal, kill, and destroy. He is coming to steal the Word from you, and he will if you let him.

Remember, the Word of God is a seed, and that seed is planted in your heart, which is your good ground. We know that in the natural it is easier to pull out a fresh seed or a plant that has no root in the ground than it is to pull up a tree or a bush that may be small, but its roots go deep in the ground so you can't pull it up. The devil's way of stealing is through problems and situations that will cause doubt and fear that will make the Word of God unproductive in your life because if you have doubt and fear, then you won't believe God's Word. Believing God's Word is faith, and if you don't have faith, you are not giving God anything to work with. Having faith in God's Word is like giving Him a key to your house when you are not there so that He can come in and fix whatever problems you have going on. If He cannot get in, then He cannot fix what you have going on. Faith is giving God the key to you; it is the way to allow Him into your life so that He can bring forth His Words so that you can receive from Him what He has already promised you.

Magnify the Word, Not the Problem

What we have to do is magnify the Word of God, not the problem. We must understand that what we see, what we have our attention on, where we are focusing our time and energy on is where our thoughts will come from, which will produce how we feel and act. "To magnify" means to enlarge, to heighten, to amplify. We need to make God's Word so big in our life that it takes all of our attention. It takes our attention off of what we are going through and puts it on what God is doing and has done for us. Also, we need to enlarge God's Word so big that we can stand behind it to where it becomes our shield. Notice, Psalm 91 tells us in verse 4 that God's truth, which is His Word, shall be our shield and buckler. Ephesians 6:16 tells us to pick up and use the shield of faith. Where does faith come from? It comes from hearing the Word of God. So, we must use the Word of God as our shield. Now you will determine the size of your shield by the amount of God's Word that you have in you. The more word and the more you focus your attention on them to magnify it, the bigger your shield will be. Now, ask yourself: do you want a shield that will only protect some of you, or would you rather have a shield big enough to protect you and your entire family? The choice is yours.

"He shall cover you with His feathers, And under His wings you shall take refuge; His truth shall be your shield and buckler" (Psalm 91:4).

"Above all, taking the shield of faith with which you will be able to quench all the fiery darts of the wicked one" (Ephesians 6:16).

Obey the Word

The reason why Joshua was so successful is that he obeyed the commands of God. The Bible was written to you and me. It is God's commands to us. I will give you an example of this. When you got saved accordingly to Romans chapter 10, you first had to believe. You believed the Word that was preached to you, and then you had to do something. You had to obey in order to be saved. What was it that you did? You confessed the Word of God. If you only believed and did not obey by confessing the Word of God, then you would have never been saved. God is clearly telling us not to let His Words depart from our eyes. If we obey this command about keeping His Words before our eyes and not letting them depart, then things will begin to change in our life. We will begin to experience more days of joy and peace; why? Because we will be more focused on His Word than we will be on the problems that surround us. It will take our focus off the things that are not true and focus our attention on the truth, the Word of God, which is our shield that we can stand behind in the midst of our storms. And His Word will protect us and allow us to come out victoriously, but we have to keep our eyes on the Word if we want to live this victorious lifestyle. Remember James 1:22. Don't be hearers only of the word, but be doers also so that you don't deceive yourself.

"But be doers of the word, and not hearers only, deceiving yourselves" (James 1:22).

Final Thought

Keeping your eyes on your promise is a must because it is a part of obeying God's commands. He tells us to keep His Words before our eyes. He wants us to write them down; He wants us to keep our focus on them because whenever we take our focus off of His Words, then we will see the lie that the enemy is trying to force on us. See, we are not only doing this for our benefit, which will keep us from worrying, from fear, from doubt, and disbelief; it will cause us to be in the perfect will of God by obeying Him. When we obey Him, then we inherit the privileges of His kingdom while we are here on earth. That is how we can live in His righteousness, we can have His joy, and we can live in His peace in the Holy Spirit because we are being led by the Spirit. His Words are the Spirit, and they are true, so when we keep our eyes on the things of the Spirit, then we will be led by the Spirit, and we will obtain spiritual things. Peter is our example to follow, so keep your eyes on God and not the storms that are going on around you. Magnify His Word so big that His Word becomes bigger than your problems, and you stand behind His Word. Let His Word become the shield that you stand and live behind, and He brings you out of the storm because, remember, He is right in the midst of the storm with you.

Chapter 9

HEAR YOUR PROMISE OVER AND OVER AND OVER

Faith Comes by Hearing

The reason we have to continue to hear God's promise for our situation over and over and over is that faith cometh by hearing, hearing the Word of God.

> "So then faith comes by hearing, and hearing by the Word of God" (Romans 10:17).

Notice, this verse does not say that faith came when you heard the word; no, it tells us that faith comes by hearing. The key to this step is that the more you hear your promise, the more faith you will build, and the stronger your faith will become. You have to be disciplined in this area. Wake up in the morning, pray, thank God for giving you another day, thank Him for supplying all of your needs today, thank Him for His protection over you and your loved ones, and thank Him for your promise, and when you say your promise out loud, then you just produced more faith. Then you get up and read it. Why? Because that is keeping your eyes on the promise, and as you read it, you say it again, and by doing that, you just produced more faith for you to make it through the day. The Word of God is just like taking medicine. When you go to the doctor, and he prescribes you medicine, you have to take it in accordance with the directions on the label. It may tell you to take it only three times a day, and it will list all of the possible side effects. Your main concern is that the medicine is going to do what it says it will do. Well, your main concern is that God's Word will do what it says it will do because His Word does not come back to Him void. The good thing about God's Word is that you can take it (meaning saying it, thinking about it, and reading it) as many times a day you want. The more you do, the better it is for you. I want to warn you that there are some side effects. The more of God you get in you, the better your life will be, the bigger the blessings will be, the better your relationship with the Father will be, and I could go on and on. Remember that you must use the same faith that you do with the medicine the doctor gave you as you do with God's Word.

Incline Your Ears

Do you remember Proverbs 4:20? Remember, it told us to incline our ears to His sayings, which are His Words. Then in verse 21, it tells us to also keep them in the midst of our heart.

"My son, give attention to my words; Incline your ear to my sayings. Do not let them depart from

your eyes; Keep them in the midst of your heart"
(Proverbs 4:20-21).

Remember Mark chapter 4, where it tells us that the
Word is a seed, and we saw that the sower sows the seed. The
sower is whoever is speaking God's Word and or preaching
and teaching God's Word, and our heart is the ground. Our
heart is the ground that Jesus is talking about. Well, to keep
God's Words in the midst of your heart, you have to put it
there by hearing the word. Then it tells you to keep it there. It
is our job, not God's job, to keep the Word within our hearts.
Just like farming, it is the farmer's job to plant the seed and
ensure it stays in the ground. So now you could ask the question, "How do we keep it there?" We keep it in the heart,
which is the good ground, by protecting it. We can protect
it in a couple of ways. One way is to keep it before our eyes
and to keep hearing it. It causes us to focus on the Word
and not on the cares of the world or the lust of the flesh.
By focusing on the word, it helps us to put the Word first.
This means that regardless of what happens, regardless if it
appears that things are changing for the worst, we must still
believe God's Word above all of those things, and it helps
when you are seeing it every day and hearing it every day. It
is a way of keeping it fresh. It keeps our focus on the good
things and not the schemes of the devil because when we focus on the schemes of the enemy, they are always contrary to
the Word of God, and they can cause us to doubt His Word.
They can cause us to fear, and fear is a big no-no when it

comes to faith in God's Word. Fear kills the seed, and faith gives the seed the nutrients it needs in order to grow. Hearing the Word produces faith, and building your faith is like watering your ground, causing it to be rich in minerals so your seed can grow. If you really want something, and you know that you are going to get it, what do you do? You will look at it or a picture of it all the time, and that is all that you will be talking about. You will keep it present in front of you at all times. We must be the same way with God's Word. He said that we could have what we say in Mark 11:23, so say His Word like it is already yours. Don't think it; know that it is yours, talk as if you already have it, and that is what faith is all about. Listen to what you are saying. Speaking the Word of God is powerful, and your stand against the enemy will depend on how much of the Word of God is in you. Believing God's Word, making it your own, and then talk and act as if it was your own is your golden ticket.

Believing

We talked about Mark 11:23, so now I want you to focus on Mark 11:24.

"Therefore I say to you, whatever things you ask when you pray, believe that you receive them, and you will have them" (Mark 11:24).

Here we see that Jesus is telling us the same thing that He said in verse 23 that we have to believe. If you don't have the faith to believe that you can have what you say, then you must go back to the simplest level that there is, and that is believing that when you pray that you can have whatever it is, you are asking God for when you pray. The key is within this verse. You have to believe first that you received it at that very moment, and then you will have it. If you believe that you have it, then you have it right. If you bought something off of eBay or Amazon and you have not even paid for it yet, but you know that it is yours. You may even start making preparations for it before it arrives. Before you even know it is in the mail, you start telling people that you have it and acting as if it is already in your possession. Well, that is how God's faith works. We have to believe that we have it now. We have to act as if we have it now. The Bible says in the book of James that faith without works is dead. Well, what are the works? I have already told you that the works are to believe. We know we got to believe with our hearts, but how do we do that? Romans chapter 10 gives us a good example of this. Let's look at verse 10.

> "For with the heart one believes unto righteousness, and with the mouth confession is made unto salvation" (Romans 10:10).

Okay, the key is within this verse. It says that when we believe with our heart, we will confess it—acting on what we believe is simply confessing it. Think about it first in the natural. Would you confess or talk about anything that you did not believe or that you could not prove to be true?

Well, that is what we have to do with the Word of God. Even the apostle Paul gives us another example of believing and speaking in 2 Corinthians 4:13. Paul tells us that he believes, and therefore he speaks.

> "And since we have the same spirit of faith, according to what is written, "I believed and therefore I spoke," we also believe and therefore speak" (2 Corinthians 4:13).

Whatever we believe God will do or has done for us, we have to confess it. The Word "confession" means to acknowledge. So what are we acknowledging? We are acknowledging that God's Word is true, that we are placing it first in our lives, and we believe with our hearts because we are confessing it over our lives. Then we walk around acting like we already have it. We begin to see ourselves with it. We start making preparations as if we already have it or making preparations because we know it is coming. Another example is when a woman is expecting a baby. The parents will go ahead to buy a car seat and a stroller. They will even buy the baby bed, a crib and maybe even dedicate one room in the house for the nursery. You see how they act because they know the baby is coming. Well, we have to act the same way when we know that God's Word is about to manifest in our lives. Confession is the key, and we will get more into confession in the next paragraph.

Confessing

Confession is important. We have to acknowledge that we agree with the Word of God and that we can put His Word first place in our lives, and we must be able to take His Word as the final authority in any situation that we are in. Confession is also translated as saying the same thing. This can be looked at in two different ways. One, we are saying the same thing that God says about us and how He sees us coming out of our situation; and the second thing is that instead of talking about your problem, giving it life, remember Proverbs 18:21 states that we speak life or death when we talk. So, stop giving your problem life. What I mean is that it has no right in your life, but if you keep talking about it, confessing it, then you are giving it a right to stay there. Let's do the smart thing and not talk about it, and then we cut off its power source, and then we begin to watch it die or remove itself because we are not giving it anything to live on. Let's start bringing God's best to our situation, and that is God's Word which we know brings life to a dead situation, which gives us the victory, which causes us to overcome. Let's continue saying the same thing over and over and over. This is confessing God's Word about our situation all the time. If we do that, it keeps us from speaking negatively about our problem, and it keeps us from giving our problem a right to stay in our life. Let's look at Hebrews 4:14.

"Seeing then that we have a great High Priest who

has passed through the heavens, Jesus the Son of God, let us hold fast our confession" (Hebrews 4:14).

This verse in some Bibles will read profession. Profession and confession mean the same thing. Let us continue to acknowledge, taking ownership, making God's Words ours, and let His Words do what they are supposed to do. Remember, His Words do not come back to Him void. We are to hold fast to saying the same thing because God's Words are our sword in the spiritual realm, according to Ephesians 6:17. So, let us continuously use our sword to drive back the enemy, to bring light into our situation, and then that is when we will see God's Word, what we believe in our heart manifest in the natural right before our eyes. Remember, the more we confess God's Word, the more faith we are building to help us endure to the end because faith comes by hearing the Word of God, and every time you make a confession, you are hearing the Word of God. You see how everything works together for our good. Praise God!

"And take the helmet of salvation, and the sword of the Spirit, which is the Word of God" (Ephesians 6:17).

Final Thought

Again, we have to keep our ears inclined to the Word

of God. It is a command, and God requires obedience over sacrifice any day. Our obedience when it comes to God's Word is like the answer to a math problem. It is either wrong or right because partial obedience is still disobedience because God gave the command to obey it fully, not partially. Plus, you need to keep hearing your promise over and over and over because it produces more faith. It builds your faith and faith believes. So, why wouldn't you do something that is going to cause you to believe God's Word? Confessing helps us more than what we know. It not only strengthens our faith every time we confess God's promises over our lives, but it also helps us to talk about how good God is, and it helps us to not talk about the problem or how bad things are around us. The Bible tells us that we need to have the Word of Christ in us richly. You may ask, "Well, why is this so important?" Jesus told us that out of the heart, the man speaks. So whatever that is in you is the very thing that is going to come out of you. So confess the Word of God. Keep speaking it because we know that faith comes by hearing the Word of God. Even when you are reading and studying the word, read it out loud so it gets down into your spirit, the real you, and then begin to listen to the real you speak. Remember, the apostle Paul said we believe therefore we speak. We, too, must believe and speak. We must agree with the Word of God the same way the apostle Paul did. We must agree with God's Word and let it be known that we agree with His Word and we thank Him for His Word, and others will see God's Word do the work. Remember, God said that the battle is not ours but His. So, speak and believe His Words and let His Words fight the battle for God. The more you speak, the more fighting words you put out there, so you determine how many fighting words you want out there on your behalf.

Chapter 10

MEDITATE ON YOUR PROMISE UNTIL YOU ARE FULL

The Word All the Time

Remember Joshua 1:8. It tells us that God told Joshua after Moses had died that he should never let the Book of the Law depart from his mouth and that he should meditate on it day and night and that he must do what it says. And if he did, he would make his own way prosperous, and he will have good success.

> This Book of the Law shall not depart from your mouth, but you shall meditate in it day and night, that you may observe to do according to all that is written in it. For then you will make your way prosperous, and then you will have good success.
>
> **Joshua 1:8**

Now, when we look at this verse, it covers our first two steps. One, he should talk about God's Words so it would produce faith and that he should meditate on it day and night.

In order for him to do this, he would have to look at the book. Can you learn anything from just carrying a book? No, you have to read the pages. God said to do this day and night, and you must obey it as well. Before we get into what meditating is, I want to show you one more scripture that we have already covered, but we were not focusing on the meditating part.

> And these words which I command you today shall be in your heart. You shall teach them diligently to your children, and shall talk of them when you sit in your house, when you walk by the way, when you lie down, and when you rise up. You shall bind them as a sign on your hand, and they shall be as frontlets between your eyes. You shall write them on the doorpost of your house and on your gates.

Deuteronomy 6:6-9

Look at how this verse starts. It starts off with God telling us that the words that they were about to hear that day shall be in their hearts. Next, God directs them to do everything they can to keep them (His Words) in their hearts and to put them in the heart of their children as well. God instructs them to talk about His Word when they were at home with their children, when they were walking with them in the streets, and even when they are about to lie down. But God does not stop there; God also tells them to talk about His Word as soon as they wake up in the morning. He instructed them to make signs so that they could see them and read them. God wanted His Word to be everywhere they were at all times. Also, God is telling us that we must become one with the word. This means that you have to keep the Word in front of you and in you at all times and that you are so full of the Word that you and the Word become one. We must reach the point where the Word will be the thing you talk about the majority of the time. You will find yourself doing the Word majority of the time because you have become the word. At this point, you have spent so much time in the Word that you have now reached true meditation.

Meditation

I want to break down meditation to the point where you will be able to understand what it means and how to be successful in your life when it comes to meditation. The first question is what we know or what we think we know about meditation. Meditation is not sitting on the floor Indian-style humming, burning candles, and whatever else goes on. No, meditation means that you mutter the Word of God to yourself. It also means to simply focus on God's Word, and the verse that explains this for us is found in 2 Peter 1:19.

"And so we have the prophetic word confirmed, which you do well to heed as a light that shines in a dark place, until the day dawns and the morning star rises in your hearts" (2 Peter 1:19).

We are told in this verse that we will do well if we keep focusing on God's Word because it is the one light that you have in any dark time or dark place as you wait for daybreak and the rising of the Morning Star in our hearts. "Meditate" means to consider or to study thoughtfully. So this verse is telling us that when we focus, I mean really focus, consider, and study His Word, there will be a rising of the Morning Star in our hearts. Now, I know you may be thinking, who is or what is the Morning Star? Well, our answer is found in the book of Revelations.

> "I, Jesus, have sent My angel to testify to you these things in the churches. I am the Root and the Offspring of David, the Bright and Morning Star" (Revelation 22:16).

> "He was clothed with a robe dipped in blood, and His name is called The Word of God" (Revelation 19:13).

In Revelation 22:16, we see that Jesus is the Morning Star. He tells us this Himself. Now, I want you to consider that if Jesus is the Morning Star, then how will Jesus rise in our hearts? The answer to this question is found in Revelation 19:13. It tells us that He (Jesus) is the Word of God. Now that we know who the Morning Star is, and we know that Jesus is called the Word of God; now we can go back to the verse in 2 Peter and get a better understanding. In 2 Peter, it is telling us that if we meditate on God's Word, we should rejoice and give thanks in any situation because we know that as we meditate on His Word, God's Word will rise up in our spirit to give us an answer, direction, joy, peace, righteousness, and strength. In the natural, if you were trying to figure out a problem, you would focus and study it until you could come up with an answer or a solution, and then, all of a sudden, you would get an idea, or you would get advice from someone who would give you some insight or an idea that would help you figure it out. Well, in the spiritual realm, it works like that, but instead of focusing on the problem, instead of focusing on the darkness of your situation, we focus on the Word of God until the Holy Spirt bears witness with our spirit and gives us God's answer, which is the true answer. His answer is the answer that will not come back void but will break through as a bright and morning light out of the darkness of night. We need to have some sort of light when we are trying to live out the will of God for us in Christ.

"Rejoice always, pray without ceasing, in everything give thanks; for this is the will of God in Christ Jesus for you" (1 Thessalonians 5:16-18).

Christ is that light, and we must follow that light, and that is how we will be able to rejoice, pray without ceasing, and give thanks regardless of what is going on around us. Psalm 119:130 tells us that the entrance of God's Words gives light; it gives understanding to the simple.

"The entrance of Your words gives light; It gives understanding to the simple" (Psalm 119:130).

Is it starting to come together for you yet? It is His Word that will enlighten us; it is His Word that will give us the insight; it is His Word that you will need in any and every situation because His Word will dawn on you, and this is all obtainable by meditating on the Word of God. This is how we will make our way successful and prosperous because the Holy Spirit will give you the answers, and He will guide you into all truth, and He will tell you all things. Not just spiritual things but all things.

> "But the Helper, the Holy Spirit, whom the Father will send in My name, He will teach you all things and bring to your remembrance all things that I said to you" (John 14:26).

> "However, when He, the Spirit of truth, has come, He will guide you into all truth; for He will not speak on His own authority, but whatever He hears He will speak; and He will tell you things to come" (John 16:13).

When you follow and obey, and "to obey" means to submit, so when we submit to God's commands within His Words, it will be easy for us to have His joy, His peace, and His righteousness, which will enable us to rejoice, pray without ceasing, and give thanks regardless of what comes in front of us because we know that we will come out with the victory, we know that we want to be in the dark, we know that our way will always be successful and prosperous because we have the Word of God. His Word will allow us to rest in it, we can look and listen at it day and night, we can focus on it and consider it, and we can allow God to come in and give us His perfect will for our lives through Christ Jesus, who is the Word of God.

Until You Are Full

The reason I am saying until you are full is the fact that the Word of God is spiritual food, and we are spiritual beings that have a soul (mind, will, and emotions), and we live in a body.

"Now may the God of peace Himself sanctify you completely; and may your whole spirit, soul, and body be preserved blameless at the coming of our Lord Jesus Christ" (1 Thessalonians 5:23).

Jesus tells us in Matthew 4:4 that man cannot live on bread alone but that he must live on every word that comes from the mouth of God. This means that we have to eat God's Word, and we do that by feeding our spirit. We do this by listening to His Word, looking at His Word, and studying His Word. Jesus also tells us that He is the bread of life and that we must eat of Him. Remember, Revelations 19:13 tells us that His name is called the Word of God, so we must eat the Word of God daily if we want to be successful in this world. Remember, Jesus told us in His example of how to pray, to ask God for our daily bread, the Word of God is what we need every day.

"But He answered and said, "It is written, Man shall not live by bread alone, but by every word that proceeds from the mouth of God" (Matthew 4:4).

Most assuredly, I say to you, he who believes in Me has everlasting life. I am the bread of life. Your fathers ate the manna in the wilderness, and are dead. This is the bread which comes down from heaven, that one may eat of it and not die. I am the living bread which came down from heaven. If anyone eats of this bread, he will live forever; and the bread that I shall give is My flesh, which I shall give for the life of the world.

John 6:47-51

In this manner, therefore, pray: Our Father in heaven, Hallowed be Your name. Your kingdom come. Your will be done On earth as it is in heaven. Give us this day our daily bread. And forgive us our debts, As we forgive our debtors. And do not lead us into temptation, But deliver us from the evil one. For Yours is the kingdom and the power and the glory forever. Amen.

Matthew 6:9-13

Now, the reason I say until you are full is that God gave me a prophetic word about what we are not doing with His Word. He told me that we, as His children, are not eating everything on our plate when it comes to His Word. God will give us a verse to help us with what we are going through, but we don't study it; we don't meditate on it until we have gotten the fullness of the revelation that is contained within the word. God told me that we just taste what is on our plate and that we need to finish what we started eating until we are full. What we are really doing is just sampling what is on our plate, then looking for another plate to eat off of, and it seems like we never find another good plate of food. The reason for this is because we have not got all of the nutrients and vitamins from the plate that was provided because we have not eaten everything that was on our plate. Remember, when I say our plate, I am talking about the verse that God has given us to help in our situation. We must study and consider that verse until the Morning Star dawns in our hearts, and then we will know the next step to take in our situation.

The Prophetic Word

Before I start, I want you to know that the Bible is the Word of God and that if anyone tells you that they received a prophetic word, make sure it agrees with the Word of God, and if it does not, then you may want to proceed with caution because the Holy Spirit will never give us anything that is contrary to God's Word for Him and God are one, so they will always say the same thing. Also, I have scripture that goes with the Word that I got from God so that you can study it for yourself and ask God to reveal the truth of the Word to you. This is the Word that I got on the night of February 13th going into the morning of the 14th. You just taste. When you pile on food, you don't eat it all. It just sits there. I give you just enough to eat a day. But you have yet to eat that. You won't get any more knowledge of your situation because you have not eaten what I have given you. Meditate on what I have given you. That is your nourishment for that day. After you have eaten that, I will give you more. There will be no more food provided to you until you eat what I have given you. You will get more after you finish your first plate. This is how you learn about how you must walk in your battle against your situation or circumstance. When you keep reading what I have given you, more meaning will come, wisdom will come, and knowledge will be provided. Don't push your plate aside looking for more; you have not eaten what I gave you; therefore, you are still in the same spot. Eat, and advance more will be given when you first eat what I have given you.

Confirmation

The great thing about God is that He goes above and beyond to let us know that His Word is true and that we can be sure of His Word. That night after I received the prophetic word, He told me that I could be as sure of this as Antonio was that day he was on his bicycle on the corner. Now I won't get into his situation, but what I can tell you is that when I stood up because I was on my knees, writing on the floor, I told him that God said I could be sure about His Word as he was sure about what happened that day when he was on the corner on his bike. He then asked me what I was talking about. I then told him I didn't know and that all I was given was him being on a bike and on the corner. Then he recalled a situation that happened that made him sure that there was a God and that God was present in his life. The next form of confirmation we got was from Joseph Prince on TBN on both the 26th and the 27th of February. Joseph Prince talked about the Lamb of God and that we must eat of that lamb. He said that we must eat till we are full, and that is when we learn. Now, the scripture that I have that will support this is in Luke 24:13-31.

Now behold, two of them were traveling that same day to a village called Emmaus, which was seven miles from Jerusalem. And they talked together of all these things which had happened. So it was, while they conversed and reasoned, that Jesus

Himself drew near and went with them. But their eyes were restrained, so that they did not know Him. And He said to them, "What kind of conversation is this that you have with one another as you walk and are sad?" Then the one whose name was Cleopas answered and said to Him, "Are You the only stranger in Jerusalem, and have You not known the things which happened there in these days?" And He said to them, "What things?" So they said to Him, "The things concerning Jesus of Nazareth, who was a Prophet mighty in deed and word before God and all the people, and how the chief priests and our rulers delivered Him to be condemned to death, and crucified Him. But we were hoping that it was He who was going to redeem Israel. Indeed, besides all this, today is the third day since these things happened. Yes, and certain women of our company, who arrived at the tomb early, astonished us. When they did not find His body, they came saying that they had also seen a vision of angels who said He was alive. And certain of those who were with us went to the tomb and found it just as the women had said; but Him they did not see." Then He said to them. "O foolish ones, and slow of heart to believe in all that the prophets have spoken! Ought not the Christ to have suffered these things and to enter into His glory?" And beginning at Moses and all the Prophets, He expounded to them in all the Scriptures the things concerning Himself. Then they drew near to the village where they were going, and He indicated that He would have gone farther. But they constrained Him, saying "Abide with us, for it is toward evening, and the day is far spent." And He went in to stay with them. Now it came to pass, as He sat at the table with them, that He took bread, blessed and broke it, and gave it to them. Then their eyes were opened and they knew Him; and He vanished from their sight.

Luke 24:13:31

Final Thought

The key here is to remain in the Word, not just remaining as reading your Bible every day but remaining on the verses that you are standing in faith on. Keeping them before your eyes, hearing them over and over, and as you keep them before your eyes, you also must consider God's Word. You must continue to study His Word. You must also continue to get everything that God has put into that promise out of that promise. If you read the Bible, then you will understand what I am talking about. You could have read a verse ten times and never got anything out of it, and then on the eleventh time, you get a revelation, and you are like, "Oh, okay, I understand it now. I know how to apply it now." Then you may go away from that verse on your quest to learn more about our heavenly Father, and then something brings you back to the verse, and you read it again, and it gives you something totally different than what you got out of it the last time. And now you are like, "Okay, I can add this to what I already have, and I can apply this to my life as well." This could happen up to two or three more times. The reason that it is happening like this is that we never got the fullness of the verse the first time. We did not remain in this verse. Remain at the verse that you are standing in faith on and watch how God continues to speak to you through this verse. Meditation is the key to unlocking all of the fullness that God has hidden within His verse. Remember, He has not hidden them from us; He has hidden them that we may find them when we really find Him.

Chapter 11

THANKSGIVING

It Is Needed

When you hear the word "thanksgiving" and how it is associated with the Bible, do you think about being in the presence of God or getting yourself in the right mental state to be in the presence of God? Do you think about gratitude towards God? Do you look at it as a gift to God from you to express your appreciation for everything that He has done in your life, what He is currently doing, and what He plans on doing? Have you ever thought to thank Him for all the things He did not allow to happen in your life and thank Him that you didn't know what was going on because that would have been something else to add to the list of things that we worry about? To refresh your memory, Psalm 95 and Psalm 100 tell us before we come into His presence, we must have thanksgiving in our hearts along with our praises because this is how we are supposed to enter into His gates.

> "Oh come, let us sing to the LORD! Let us shout joyfully to the Rock of our salvation. Let us come before His presence with thanksgiving; Let us shout joyfully to Him with psalms" (Psalm 95:1-2).

Make a joyful shout to the LORD, all you lands! Serve the LORD with gladness; Come before His presence with singing. Know that the LORD, He is God; It is He who has made us, and not we ourselves; We are His people and the sheep of His pasture. Enter into His gates with thanksgiving, And into His courts with praise. Be thankful to Him, and bless His name. For the LORD is good; His mercy is everlasting, And His truth endures to all generations.

Psalm 100

Thanksgiving is big in God's eyes, and it has to be in ours also if we want to receive God's will for us in Christ Jesus. Let's look at 1 Thessalonians 5:16-18 again.

"Rejoice always, pray without ceasing, in everything give thanks; for this is the will of God in Christ Jesus for you" (1 Thessalonians 5:16-18).

It tells us that in everything, we are to give thanks, so that means during the good times and in the bad times. It means we have to give thanks when things are easy and when rough times come. Why? Because we can enter into His presence, we can bring Him on the scene because He wants to be there, and we need Him to be there with us. We need Him there, and when we truly love Him, we won't know how to go on or go anywhere without Him being there, so we must learn to stick close to Him. We must learn how to follow Him, knowing that He will lead us down the path of righteousness for His name's sake. We saw how when the people in the Old Testament praised God and when they did, it brought Him on the scene, and when God came on the scene, He showed up and showed out.

Thanksgiving Opens the Door to Salvation

Look at what the psalmist tells us in Psalm 50:14-15, 23.

"Offer to God thanksgiving, And pay your vows to the Most High. Call upon Me in the day of trouble; I will deliver you, and you shall glorify Me" (Psalm 50:14-15).

"Whoever offers praise glorifies Me; And to him who orders his conduct aright I will show the salvation of God" (Psalm 50:23).

It tells us to offer up to God thanksgiving and pay our vows to the Most High. This is our voluntary personal dedication of devotion to God. It also tells us as we offer up our gift of thanksgiving to God that we can call on Him in the day of trouble, and He will deliver us, and we shall glorify Him. Glorify God by obeying Him, by admiring Him, pointing out all the good that's in Him and in His Word, recognize

Him as being glorious. Now, verse 23 tells us that whoever, and we are the "whoever," offers praise of thanksgiving, glorifies God, and when we do this, it puts us on the road to His righteousness, which causes us to live in obedience. When this takes place, then God will show us His salvation. This is exactly what we saw with Jehoshaphat when they started praising and thanking God for their victory. When they did this, they were able to witness His salvation.

Thanksgiving It Is Our Sacrifice

Next, let's look at Hebrews 13:15.

"Therefore by Him let us continually offer the sacrifice of praise to God, that is, the fruit of our lips, giving thanks to His name" (Hebrews 13:15).

It tells us to offer up continuous sacrifices of praise to God by giving thanks to His name. Psalm 23:3 says that He leads us in the path of righteousness for His name's sake.

"He restores my soul; He leads me in the paths of righteousness For His name's sake" (Psalm 23:3).

We give thanks for His name, Amen. God's name is holy, His name is above all names, and God will move mountains for His name's sake. In the book of Joshua, we see that Joshua understood God's name. Look at how Joshua talked with the *Lord* and asked Him what He was going to do for His name's sake because they were not going out to fight in their own name. They were going out to fight under His name.

> Now Joshua sent men from Jericho to Ai, which is beside Beth Aven, on the east side of Bethel, and spoke to them, saying, "Go up and spy out the country." So the men went up and spied out Ai. And they returned to Joshua and said to him, "Do not let all the people go up, but let about two or three thousand men go up and attack Ai. Do not weary all the people there, for the people of Ai are few." So about three thousand men went up there from the people, but they fled before the men of Ai. And the men of Ai struck down about thirty-six men, for they chased them from before the gate as far as Shebrim, and struck them down on the descent; therefore the hearts of the people melted and became like water. Then Joshua tore his clothes, and fell to the earth on his face before the ark of the LORD until evening, he and the elders of Israel; and they put dust on their heads. And Joshua said, "Alas, LORD GOD, Why have You brought this people over the Jordan at all-to deliver us into the hand of the Amorites, to destroy us? Oh, that we had been content, and dwelt on the other side of the Jordan! O LORD, what shall I

say when Israel turns its back before its enemies? For the Canaanites and all the inhabitants of the land will hear it, and surround us, and cut off your name from the earth. Then what will You do for Your great name?"

Joshua 7:2-9

Of course, one man had sinned against God, and God does not look upon us when we are covered in sin, and sin will put us in a position where we cannot receive from God. This is why Jesus said when we pray to forgive; don't keep that sin in your life because if you do, you will not receive anything from God. God told Joshua what happened, they handled the situation, got back in right standing with God, and God showed them what He would do for His name. So, praise God for His name, thank God for His name because it is because of His name that we have authority in the world; it is because of His name that we are saved, redeemed, and justified. It is by His name that we walk in victory, and all our needs are met because of His name, for He is the great "*I am.*" Whatever we need in this world, God says, "*I am.*" Thank God for His name; praise God for His name for it is good, and that is why we are on the path to righteousness. Forget about what is in front of you and give it to God, then give thanks to because you know He heard you, and He will not only do it for you because you are His child but because of His name's sake. Thank God for all that He has done in your life. Thank God for all the things that He is doing in your life right now, both seen and unseen, because we know He works all things out for our good because we love Him. Thank God because what the enemy meant to hurt you, God has turned it around for your good.

Pray and Give Thanks

The apostle Paul tells us in Philippians 4:4-7:

Rejoice in the Lord always. Again I will say, rejoice! Let your gentleness be known to all men. The Lord is at hand. Be anxious for nothing, but in everything by prayer and supplication, with thanksgiving, let your requests be made known to God; and the peace of God, which surpasses all understanding, will guard your hearts and minds through Christ Jesus.

Philippians 4:4-7

Thanksgiving helps us to draw from God's peace because it reminds us of how good He has been to us, how He has pulled us out of the mud before, and how He puts us back on dry ground. It's things like this that cause us to have peace. God's peace is the peace that will guard our minds and our hearts, so thank God for His name's sake, His righteousness, His grace, and His mercy. Paul also tells us again to pray and give thanks in Colossians 4:2.

"Continue earnestly in prayer, being vigilant in it with thanksgiving" (Colossians 4:2).

Pray, watch, and give thanks. God's Word tells us to give thanks always for all things to God. Give thanks because God is faithful and watch for God's goodness and His light to start to break through the darkness of your situation and provide the way of escape for Jesus said that He is the way, the truth, and the life.

"Giving thanks always for all things to God the Father in the name of our Lord Jesus Christ" (Ephesians 5:20).

"Jesus said to him, "I am the way, the truth, and the life. No one comes to the Father except through Me" (John 14:6).

Final Thought

Remember how we had to magnify the Word of God. Well, God and His Word are one and the same, so we must magnify God. We must magnify His name, His love, and His mercy. We honor Him when we thank Him for all of His goodness and His loving kindness. Thank Him for being a great Father. Let us bless Him and His name as we praise Him and give thanks to Him for the great things that He has done for us. Thanksgiving is also saying, "God, I believe."

Even if I can't see it yet or hold it yet, I am going to thank you for it because I believe you heard me, and I believe that I received it from you when I asked for it in prayer. Now, would you thank someone for something that they have not done? So, giving thanks to God is saying, "yes, I believe." It is part of your faith. It can make or break your faith. This is why you can rejoice because faith says you have it now. And as you begin to thank Him, gladness, which is a fruit of the spirit, will begin to bubble up on the inside of you, and without even knowing it, you will be rejoicing and praising God because His mercy and love truly endure forever.

Chapter 12

PRAY FOR OTHERS

Measure God's Word

We have to understand that how we measure God's Word will determine how it will be measured back to us. Jesus tells us this in the book of Luke, chapter 6.

> "Judge not, and you shall not be judged. Condemn not, and you shall not be condemned. Forgive, and you will be forgiven. Give, and it will be given to you; good measure pressed down, shaken together, and running over will be put into your bosom. For with the same measure that you use, it will be measured back to you."

> **Luke 6:37-38**

When I first heard of this verse, it was associated with giving so that you may receive. I understood the principle, and I thought nothing more of it. I knew that when I wanted to talk about receiving, I had a verse that tells us to give. And the measure that you give it with it will be measured back to you. Then one day, I was reading the entire chapter, and I notice that it said if we don't want to be judged, then don't judge, and if we don't want to be condemned, then don't condemn the next man. Then I noticed that it said that if I want to be forgiven, then I had to forgive. I noticed that I had to act a certain way for things to affect me. If I didn't want bad to come back to me, then I must not do these things to others. If I wanted good things to happen for me, then I had to do good unto others. Then I noticed that God was in control of my return. If I do good things to people, my return will not come from people; it will come from God. If I did bad things to people, then God would allow the bad to come back to me. It is reaping what you are sowing. Then God spoke to me, "I have given you the revelation of verses to help you with your deliverance, but there are others who are still spiritually blind, and because of their blindness, they cannot see my word the way you have. I have created you to be their light, so the same way you prayed for my promises to come to pass in your life, I want you to pray for others. I need you to pray for those who are going through the same thing that you are going through, and it will be returned to you. Also, I need you to pray for others as you see what they need in their life. When you see that they cannot grasp the revelation of my word as you speak my word to them, then you must go and pray for them in this area." I had never looked at this verse in that way, but it could easily say, "Pray for others, and with the same measure, you use my word it will return to you." Then it hit me. If I want God to do this for me, then I should start praying for others because if this is God's will for my life, then this is His will for all of our lives. I understood the fight that we were in. I started studying this, and sure enough, I found my starting point with Kenneth Copeland, and he was talking about the man in the gap. This is where my knowledge of intercessory prayer would begin.

The Man in the Gap

The man in the gap helped me to understand that when people are blind to the truths in God's Word or they simply just don't know, then we, who know, must stand in the gap for them in order for God to move on their behalf.

> The people of the land have used oppressions, committed robbery, and mistreated the poor and needy; and they wrongfully oppress the stranger. So I sought for a man among them who would make a wall, and stand in the gap before Me on behalf of the land, that I should not destroy it; but I found no one.

Ezekiel 22:29-30

The Bible tells us that the trials that we are going through are the same type of trials that our brothers and sisters in Christ are going through. The enemy does not have any new strategies, so we must understand that when we have figured out the way of escape, which is Jesus, and Jesus is the Word of God, then we have to stand on what the Word says. When we pray and believe that we received from God, then we must tell our testimony so that others can hear it and they can follow our example for their own deliverance. For some, it won't be that easy. Even with your testimony and you showing them the Word of God, they still will not be able to receive because they are unable to believe. That is when you and I have to go before God on their behalf. We are all in a spiritual war, and we have to fight spiritually. And for those who can't fight for themselves or don't know how to fight for themselves, then we have to go to war for them.

> "You have not gone up into the gaps to build a wall for the house of Israel to stand in battle on this day of the LORD" (Ezekiel 13:5).

When the battle comes for whoever we are praying for to be delivered, then we want a wall to be around them so they can be protected and that they can come out of the battle with the victory that God has promised to all of us through Christ Jesus. We have to be the man or woman in the gap. Some people may think, "Well, when I start praying for other people, the enemy will turn up the heat on me." I am here to tell you he can try, but he won't be successful because as you intercede on another's behalf, you are protected. We find this truth also in the book of Ezekiel and in the book of Luke.

> And the LORD said to him, "Go through the midst of the city, through the midst of Jerusalem, and put a mark on the foreheads of the men who sigh and cry over all the abominations that are done

within it." To the others He said in my hearing, "Go after him through the city and kill; do not let your eye spare, nor have any pity. Utterly slay old and young men, maidens and little children and women; but do not come near anyone on whom is the mark; and began at My sanctuary."

Ezekiel 9:4-6

"Behold, I give you the authority to trample on serpents and scorpions, and over all the power of the enemy, and nothing shall by any means hurt you" (Luke 10:19).

We see the one who went out did not go out alone. When you are interceding for others, you are protected because you are doing God's work. God's will is for everyone to be saved. His will for His sons and daughters in Christ Jesus is for them to have life and have it more abundantly and for us to continue to live in victory. For those who are blinded, you are standing in faith on their behalf, and they will be spared, they will be able to receive God's salvation, and the entire time you will be protected, nothing shall by any means hurt you, and the measure that you used it will be measured back unto you.

Intercession Changes Things

The apostle Paul encourages us all to intercede for all

151

people, not just brothers and sisters in Christ but for all people.

> "Therefore I exhort first of all that supplications, prayers, intercessions, and giving of thanks be made for all men" (1 Timothy 2:1).

Paul even tells us to pray for those who are in leadership as well because if we want to live life without constant oppression, then we have to pray for those who are in a position to oppress. I like how Kenneth Copeland puts it. He states: "That intercession is twofold. We can approach a merciful God with a plea or petition for mercy, and we can approach the enemy (never the person) on behalf of another. Jesus did this for us, and He still does it for us now. And you can read about it in the book of Isaiah chapter 59, and it also tells us about it in Isaiah 53 and Hebrews 7.

> Therefore I will divide Him a portion with the great, And He shall divide the spoil with the strong, Because He poured out His soul unto death, And He was numbered with the transgressors, And He bore the sin of many, And made intercession for the transgressors.
>
> **Isaiah 53:12**

> "Therefore He is also able to save to the uttermost those who come to God through Him, since He always lives to make intercession for them" (Hebrews 7:25).

"Now He who searches the hearts knows what the mind of the Spirit is, because He makes intercession for the saints according to the will of God" (Romans 8:27).

Jesus interceded for us in the past, and He still intercedes for us now at the right hand of the Father. Also, the Holy Spirit is interceding on our behalf as well. This is a clear indication that intercession is needed, and it is a force to be reckoned with when it is used by the believer. We have to intercede for others who don't have the ability to go before God for themselves and for those that don't know how to fight the devil off and how to properly use their authority that has been given to them. It is amazing how you will start to see things manifest in your life when you begin standing in the gap for others. In one of Kathryn Kuhlman's books, I read a lady testimony where she was bound to a wheelchair, and she wanted to heal, but she wanted her boss to accept Jesus as his Lord and Savior more than she wanted her healing. She prayed for her boss and asked God to save him. They both went to Kathryn's healing meeting, and as her boss was accepting Jesus Christ into his heart, she was instantly healed. Talk about God's measure returning to us. Remember, He can do more than we can ever ask or think.

Final Thought

Remember, when God wanted something, He gave. He

wanted mankind back, so He gave the only Son that He had and in return. Look at how many sons and daughters He has now, not to mention He did not lose Jesus and that Jesus is right back with Him, sitting at the right hand of God. I said that to say this. When you think you are losing something, you are not; you are just planting what you have trusted God with it. Remember the young lad with the five loaves and two fish. He gave Jesus all he had, and in return, he left with twelve baskets. We have to trust God that He has us and turn some of our attention off of ourselves and pray for those we love. Pray for those who are lost. We must pray for those who are lost and for our brothers and sisters in Christ but have not obtained the truth in God's Word, so we have to stand in the gap for them so that God can move on their behalf. And when we do this, we have to know that God got us and that He will take care of them too because we believed, and therefore, we stood in the gap for them. If we ever get the revelation that God supplies all of our needs so that we can help those who don't know, then and only then will we begin to start living the abundant life. I must know that I lack nothing, and whatever it is I think I need, God will provide it because it is not for me to use it all on myself but to share with my brothers and sisters in need. It teaches us to get rid of our selfishness mentally and get the mind of Christ, and then we will begin to see more breakthroughs in our own lives.

Chapter 13

PRAY IN THE SPIRIT

What Is Praying in the Spirit

Praying in the Spirit is praying in tongues. A lot of people still don't believe in this, but it is in the Bible. I don't understand how we as people can pick and choose what we want to believe and not believe when it comes to the Bible. The baptism in the Holy Spirit with the evidence of speaking in tongues is real. If you are not praying in the Spirit, you are missing out on God's best for you, and you are missing out on a chance to strengthen your spirit, man, which is the real you. Let's look at the reasons why we have to pray in the Spirit.

The Root Cause

We are praying and asking God to remove something out of our life, or we could be asking to be delivered from something. Well, that certain something could be a symptom of the real problem and not the root cause. Even with medicines, we always fight by what symptoms we have. Well, what if we have a fever along with a running nose, headaches, and two or three other symptoms. Now, we can take aspirin that may get rid of the fever temporarily, and the headache may leave, but we still have other stuff going on. Until we find out the root cause, such as the flu, a sinus infection, or just a common cold, we won't be able to truly get rid of the real problem. The same thing holds true for the spiritual world. What we are going through may not be the root of our troubles; it could be something else. Something like unconfessed sin, unforgiveness, not walking in love, but what we are going through could be a financial problem, sickness, or relationships that are falling apart. So, we will pray for God to help us in these areas, but what we really need is to repent, forgive, or walk in love. Once we fix the root cause, we get back to obeying God and walking upright with Him, and when we do this, everything else will have to get in line or flee because we have submitted ourselves to God. And when we do that, the devil and the mess he brings has to flee. I will tell you how praying in the Spirit helps us with this, but let me give you a Bible example of what I am talking about. In the book of Nehemiah chapter one, the survivors, who were left from the captivity in the province, were in great distress and reproach, plus the wall of Jerusalem has been broken down, and its gates had been burned with fire. So, on the outside looking in, their problem looked like they needed to pray to be delivered from captivity and for Jerusalem to be re-built. But from the inside looking out (the Holy Spirit is inside and knows the perfect will of God for your life), Nehemiah went to God to seek the answer to all that was going on, and he found out that the root cause, the main reason for what was going on, was because of the unconfessed sins of not only his father but their forefathers, and it was the children's of Israel sins that were causing these things to happen. When Nehemiah asked for the forgiveness of their sins, God not only allowed them but gave them everything they needed, plus provided protection to which allowed them to rebuild the wall, and those in captivity were allowed to return.

This Is Our Weakness

The Bible tells us that one of our weaknesses is the fact that we don't know what we should pray for, but the Spirit does and intercedes on our behalf.

> Likewise the Spirit also helps in our weaknesses. For we do not know what we should pray for as we ought, but the Spirit Himself makes intercession for us with groanings which cannot be uttered. Now He who searches the hearts knows what the mind of the Spirit is, because He makes intercession for the saints according to the will of God.

Romans 8:26-27

We can rejoice to know that with our natural minds, we would never know how to pray God's plan and His thoughts towards us, but the Holy Spirit knows the plans that God has for us because He has been there since the beginning. Paul tells us in Corinthians that only the spirit of God knows the things of God, and the same spirit is within us, ready to intercede for us according to the will of God. See, the Holy Spirit knows the will of God for our life, and it will deal with the root cause and give us the revelation so that we may do what is needed for us to begin to walk upright with God.

To Build Us Up

In 1 Corinthians chapter 14, it tells us some important things to know when it comes to praying in tongues. It tells us in verse two that we speak mysteries to God. It is no mystery to God because God and His spirit know all things. It is a mystery to us because we are not praying in our natural tongue using words from our natural mind; it is the Holy Spirit doing the talking. Then in verse 4, it tells us that whoever prays in tongues edifies himself. "To edify" means to build up, to encourage, to strengthen, and to unify. Who wouldn't want to build themselves up, encourage themselves, and strengthen themselves?

"For he who speaks in a tongue does not speak to men but to God, for no one understands him; however, in the spirit he speaks mysteries" (1 Corinthians 14:2).

"He who speaks in a tongue edifies himself, but he who prophesies edifies the church" (1 Corinthians).

See, when we pray in the Spirit, we don't build up or strengthen our physical selves; no, we build up our spiritual selves, the real us. Look at Jude 1:20 with me.

"But you, beloved, building yourselves up on your most holy faith, praying in the Holy Spirit" (Jude 1:20).

Again, we see we build ourselves up on our most holy faith by praying in the Spirit. This means as we pray in the Spirit, we strengthen our spirit and build ourselves up until our spirit begins to dominate our flesh, and our faith will go higher and higher as well. It will help with our faith because we will be praying God's will into our lives, and we will strengthen our faith because of the revelations and knowledge the Spirit will give to us. Then God has not stopped there. Even though we speak mysteries, they don't have to stay a mystery. Verse 13 in 1 Corinthians chapter 14 tells us to pray in our natural tongue to interpret what we are praying in the Spirit so that we can agree with it and confess it and pray again in our natural tongue.

"Therefore let him who speaks in a tongue pray that he may interpret" (1 Corinthians 14:13).

It's a Command

In Ephesians chapter six, it tells us to put on the whole

armor of God, and in verse 18, it tells us to pray always in the Spirit, and to watch, to stay alert, be ready to move on God's commands, be ready to combat the devil lies, and also we can pray for other saints when we pray in the Spirit. God may need you to intercede for someone you don't even know. You will just fill a need to go and pray. There have been countless times this has happened, and people prayed, then found out later they had prayed for someone who was in time of need, and God moved on their behalf.

Final Thought

As we have come to the last step, we must consider this step just as important as the rest of them; because it is numbered last does not mean that if you don't make it to this step, then you don't have to do it. This step is a must in your life every day, whether things are going good or they are going bad. We need this every day because we can be tempted at any time, any day. So in order for your spirit to dominate your flesh, who wants to be in control, you will have to strengthen your spirit man every chance you get. Plus, you will be praying God's will not only for your life but for that day. We don't know what each day holds, but the Holy Spirit does. So why not let Him intercede for you and another saint if it is God's will for that day. You can't lose by doing it, so why not take advantage of another tool that God has given us to trample the devil under our feet.

Chapter 14
MY TESTIMONY/STAND ON SATURDAYS

My Testimony

Okay, there are a lot of testimonies I can use, but this one that I am choosing to share here helped to increase my faith tremendously, and it showed me how I had a revelation of God's Word in this area and not so strong or not at all in other areas, which lead me to get into the Word in those areas so that I could get the revelation of them as well. My baby boy, the youngest of all my kids, was born with low iron. I think I'm not for sure, but the limit is twelve, and when it is under ten, they begin to get concerned. Well, his was at an eight point nine, sometimes a nine point something, but never higher than ten. So when I was arrested, my son's iron was still low, and they had him on medicine, which was iron in a liquid form. All of a sudden, he kept getting really bad colds. His mother would take him to the doctor, and they would say it was his asthma, or it was bronchitis or an upper respiratory infection. They would give him antibiotics. They also gave him an inhaler, breathing treatments, I mean, they gave him the works, but he never got better. So I told my wife that I believed that by Jesus stripes, he was healed. Now here is where the problem was. As a concerned father, every day, I would show signs of worrying by trying to show my wife that I was concerned, so every day we talked, I would ask her if he was better, and the answer was always no. Then one day, God spoke to me and said that it is not faith when I ask every day and that I was looking for a sign to believe, and then He said, "Just give it to me and believe." So I told my wife about the situation, and I told her I cared, but I was not going to ask if he was healed anymore. About two weeks after that phone call, it was time for his iron to be re-filled. When my wife went to get the medicine, it had been recalled. So my wife being the investigator that she is, see that is a much better word for being noisy. She went to the website of the product and noticed that it could cause upper respiratory infections. So in two weeks, he was completely healed. So when my wife took him for his next check-up, she was expecting his iron to be super low because nothing else had been prescribed. So after the check-up, the doctor came in and said everything was good and that we were free to leave. So my wife asked about his iron. The doctor said that his iron was fine; it was at a fourteen point something, I believe, and it has been normal ever since. God is so good! He not only healed my son of the upper respiratory infection, but He also healed him from the low iron as well. He not only healed my son but made him whole. We also broke the generational curse of breast cancer that was on my wife's side of the family. Notice, I said it was because we broke the curse.

An Example of Sharing My Testimony

This is a different situation. I was about to start writing my next Bible study lesson, and as I was sitting down, I started having all kinds of crazy symptoms. My head started pounding, my vision was blurry, I felt sick, and I thought I was going to pass out. I said to myself, "Now, I know God would not keep me from His Word, so this must be from the devil." I remember saying whatever this is, I don't want it, and it does not belong to me, and I rebuke it in the name of Jesus. Instantly, all the symptoms left, and I wrote out my lesson. When I finished, Damien from Texas was coming out of his cell, and I told him what had happened. He stated that his wife had been going through some of the same things and was currently at the hospital. He said, "Let me call her to find out what's going on and to tell her to do that." Well, that previous Sunday, she had helped out with Sunday school and did such a great job they asked her would she be willing to take a class and run it herself. This was on Tuesday, and she said yes. Now it was Saturday, and she had been dealing with these symptoms since Tuesday. She had dealt with it as long as she could, and now she was in the ER. So as she told Damien this, it hit him. Man Jack just went through the same thing. See, the devil did not want her to do God's work, and Damien realized it. Right there on the phone together, they rebuked the devil, and her symptoms left her instantly. She still got checked out, and the doctors could not find anything wrong with her.

Witness to a Miracle

Remember my friend Terrance. Well, his daughter was in a really bad car accident. She was in a coma when they arrived on the scene and was in a coma when Terrance got the news. We prayed about it and agreed that by Jesus stripes, she was healed (Isaiah 53:5, 1 Peter 2:24) and that we could have what we said and that we had to believe that we received when we prayed (Mark 11:23-24). We were detained at the time, so Terrance said, "I have to go home to pray over my daughter and lay hands on her, and my faith will get her to receive her healing." Well, things that don't happen and things that never happen began to happen. Terrance was never given a bond, but the judge allowed him to leave and go home for two days to be with his daughter. He prayed over her and laid hands on her, and believed. While he was there, he had told his family that he was going to join the church. Well, he went to church, and as they were starting, all the lights were deemed, and when they came back on, the entire church was blue. He asked his mother if she had remembered the dream that he had six months earlier. He had told her about his dream, and he had told other inmates about him being in a church, and the entire church lighting was blue. After the two days, Terrance had to come back, and it seemed like things were getting worst with his daughter. The doctors had called the family in to tell them that his daughter was not going to make it. When he called home that day, his mother was crying and telling him everything that the doctors had said. Terrance told his mother that she had to believe, and he didn't care what the doctors said; God told him that his daughter would not die. The very next day, the doctors called the family in and told them that they were sorry and that they didn't know what happened, but all her tests were fine and that they were about to start performing some of the surgeries that she needed. Her story is not over, but when I finished writing this book, his daughter was at home talking to her father on the phone after the doctors told her family it was over with, but Terrance stood on what God said, and his daughter is still here today with him. Give God the glory!

Stand on Saturdays

"Stand on Saturdays" started why I was detained by the federal government. For those of us in our Bible Study group, we all knew the importance of confession. When we confess God's Word, we strengthen our faith because faith comes by hearing the Word of God, and we also show that we agree with His Word, we are acknowledging His word in our life, and that His Word is the first place in our lives, and it is the final word in our situation. So we had this thing that we would do where we would walk up to each other and ask each other what you are standing on. Of course, we were standing on God's Word, but we would have to tell the other person the verse. We made each verse our own, and that is what we stood on. We would confess the verse to the other person and tell the other person where the verse was. For example, if a person needed healing and they believed that they had received their healing, they would say, "I am standing on 1 Peter 2:24 because, by Jesus stripes, I am healed." It not only helped us to learn and know and believe God's Words in our hearts, but it also helped us to magnify God's Word by focusing on His Word, and it kept us from talking so much about our situation. It caused us to stop giving our situation life, and this helped us out tremendously.

CONCLUSION

We now know that faith is the substance of things hoped for. Now, we have to ask ourselves what we are hoping for. The promises of God that are throughout the Bible are what we should be hoping for, and then we must turn that hope into faith. Faith is the evidence of things not seen. If you are standing in faith for something as you are reading this book, you are probably going through something that contradicts what the Word of God says. This means what you are hoping for is unseen because what you are going through is what is in front of your face. It may be so close to your face that you can't see anything else but that. But God said, "My promises that you have found are the evidence of what you can't see, so look at my promises day and night, for my promises are my words." And Jesus is the living word of God, and He is the way out of your problem; He is the truth in your situation because your situation is a lie; it is a shadow before your face to force you to give up and turn away in defeat. I am telling you that when you start to believe that Jesus is the way out that He is your answer, now you just turned your hope into faith, and then you can start thanking God for answering your prayer and continue to focus on your answer until the evidence of what was not seen has manifested in your life. And now everyone sees it, and you are giving God the glory. Remember, Jesus, the Word of God, is showing us the truth of how God sees us in our situations. Jesus is life, life is light, and He is the light that will lead us out of darkness, so keep your eyes on the light. We know we must live by faith, walk by faith, and it is impossible to please God without faith, but just seeing God's Words and knowing what God says about your situation is not enough. You and I have to get His Word down in our hearts. We must keep speaking and reading His Word until we start to believe, not with our mind but with our heart, and then we will start living as if we already have it, and that is what faith is all about. We have to live it, speak it, tell ourselves and everyone around us, for the Word of God says we will be witnesses of our Lord and Savior Jesus Christ. Some people will say, "Well, you don't have it now, so really you are lying." You are not lying; you have just come to the point of you understanding how faith works. Faith is not pretending that what we are going through is not real or that these situations don't exist. No, faith is agreeing with what God has said about your situation. God has given us all the same measure of faith, so it is time for us to start using what God has put in us. Remember, if He has given it to us, then it is needed; and He would not have given it to us if we were not able to use it. We must use our faith the way God uses it. Romans 4:17 tells us that God gives life to the dead and calls those things which do not exist as though they did. When we start speaking God's Word about our situation, we will not be telling lies; we will simply be speaking faith, and when we do this, we will be speaking life into our dark or dead situation. In Genesis chapter one, the Bible tells us that the earth was dark and without form. When God spoke,

He did not say that the earth was dark and without form. He did not say anything about how the earth was; He just spoke things that were not as though it was already there. He said, "Let there be light," and there was light. Now ask yourself, did God lie? No, because it is impossible for Him to lie; He just spoke what He wanted to see, and it happened. God wants to see a certain outcome for your life and your current situation. So, find out what it is, believe it, and continue to speak that and only that until you see it and may God bless you and your family and thank Him for supplying all of your needs every day because that is who He is.

YOUR TESTIMONY

There are pages provided for you to write your own testimony. Revelation 12:11 tells us that we overcame him (meaning the evil one) by the blood of the Lamb (which is Jesus) and by our testimony. People can find things to argue about in the Bible, but no one can argue with you about your testimony, so write it down not only for yourself but share it with family, friends, church members, and even your next-door neighbor. Help this book be a blessing to others by adding your testimony. The people who are around you don't know me, but they know you, and it will make this book even more powerful because they know you and they can relate to you, and they can see you; and guess, who are you to them? The evidence that was not seen, you have become the substance that you were hoping for, and they can see, touch, and hold you. You know what you are; you are the Word of God-made flesh.

ABOUT THE AUTHOR

Adrian Jackson is the founder of Kingdom Playbook Ministries. He is a husband and father of seven as well as a Navy veteran. Adrian is also known by those closest to him as "Minister Jack" or "Coach Jack." He is a well-known football coach and has earned a Master of Science in Sports Management as well as a Bachelor of Science in Sports and Health Science. Adrian gave his life to Christ in 1997, and God has taken him on a most unusual journey to prepare him for his calling. Since he answered the call, his teachings have helped those who have heard him grow in their relationship with God, which has increased their faith. At the heart of his teachings, God put it on his heart to write a book, to help people to believe God, and to start living by faith. For Adrian, it has been life-changing as he has written several soon-to-be-published manuscripts. Adrian has witnessed firsthand how God has used what he has written to open the eyes and ears of many, which has led to many victories in the lives of others as well as one of his most heartfelt victories.

CPSIA information can be obtained
at www.ICGtesting.com
Printed in the USA
LVHW022223150721
692785LV00010B/769